A Life in Motion

A Life in Motion

Lynn Flanagan

ISBN-13: 9781981832491
ISBN-10: 1981832491

HERO
OF THE 2011 MARATHON

LYNN FLANAGAN

The positive impact Lynn has made in the lives of so many in the Tri-City Medical Center Carlsbad Marathon, the community and beyond is staggering. More than half-a-million adults and children have crossed In Motion events' finish lines. Millions of dollars have been raised for charities. Tens of thousands of people have had their lives forever changed and enriched because of the many physical and emotional benefits of exercise, camaraderie and sense of accomplishment derived from training for, and finishing, In Motion events.

Lynn with husband, Travis.

But Lynn is not a numbers person. She is a people person. Just ask the Birnbaums - the family who inspired the Spirit of Joshua Award. Or ask the Heroes honored this, or in past, years. Just ask anybody who has ever met Lynn or heard her talk about what motivates and moves her.

"I've been able to work with my family by my side, get to know so many wonderful people, raise millions of dollars for very important causes, play a role in creating events that have become landmarks and know that our work has had a positive impact on our little part of the world."

As she ever-so-slowly eases into semi-retirement, we are humbled to honor Lynn, to thank her and to name her as an official Hero of the Marathon.

Travis & Lynn

..........Emotional and Inspirational

"In this day of empowering change for women, here's a chance to see the living history of a woman who had to carve her own path through a world dominated by men. Lynn Flanagan set an example with her business and created a legacy picked up by her children while showing a graceful resilience when faced with new, life-changing challenges. It's a timely story about a great San Diegan who has touched tens of thousands. Whether they really know it or not."

Carlo Cecchetto, CBS News Anchor

"Lynn Flanagan is truly among the pioneers in the running and racing community. Her journey is filled with peaks, valleys, laughs, and tears. As you turn the pages I have no doubt that you too will be intrigued and impressed with this Life In Motion."

Rudy Novotny, Race Announcer

"We all have a story. And Lynn's especially, is a story of courage and a story of inspiration for us all. When the odds are seemingly insurmountable, she doesn't give in, she doesn't give up, she takes action and keeps moving forward."

Marilouse Micuda, La Jolla Hotel Owner

"Lynn's honesty reminds me I am not alone in my own hardships. The strength she exhibits gives me a new level to aspire to. Role models like Lynn have empowered me to accomplish my dreams, graduating from Berkeley and becoming a software engineer at a major feature film studio. She is a remarkable human being. Anyone who knows her story can't help but be inspired to be remarkable in their own life."

Kadie Jaffe, Granddaughter

"Lynn Flanagan offers us the story of courage, inspiration, and dedication. This book is an honest look at her life and the difficulties that compelled her to create a thriving fitness business. When she had nowhere to turn she looked within and found the strength to persevere. Through her personal creativity and the support of her family and friends, Lynn shows us that anything is possible. But most importantly, we find encouragement to remain committed to personal growth and improvement in the face of ongoing challenges as Lynn so courageously exemplifies."

Matt Miller, Former Standford University
Rowing Team Captain

"All I can say is WOW! You would never know that Lynn had been through any of that! I have always admired her for her calm and level attitude, but now I am in total awe of her! Incredible!"

Melanie Faulkner, Berkeley Graduate, Entrepreneur

"There are few things greater then a good read... One is a meaningful read. That's what I saw in Lynn Flanagan's book - current, inspirational, motivational, and well written, a personal story that relates to all of us in our own personal ways as a wife, mother, grandmother, business owner and officially a psychologist and rehabilitation counselor. Lynn's memoir reminded me to run forward in life leaving footprints behind for others to be inspired to follow."

Carol Goodell, Business Owner

"As a former athlete myself, I cannot help but admire Lynn Flanagan's ability to carve out a life and career surrounding a sport that she loves, and her innovativeness to get it done. Her story provides an insightful view of many of the challenges that are faced in life itself as well as those that are tackled in organizing and managing the large In Motion events. Lynn's tenacity, patience and compassion shine through."

Ellen Kasari, Texas A&M University, Veterinary Medicine

"Lynn's heartfelt words will both inspire and touch the hearts of many people. The world will be a better place. A beautiful legacy…"

Dave Chelesnik, Business Owner

Prologue

From the time I was a small child, I loved reading and writing. I was only seven when I found a copy of William Saroyan's *Human Comedy*. I was intrigued with the title, thinking, it must be fun; maybe it's a children's book. An elderly couple who lived down the road had a small collection of books available to their summer tourists. They agreed to let me borrow the *Human Comedy*. It was not what I anticipated, nor did I like it, but I had made up my mind to read it. It took me most of the summer to get through it, and I'm quite sure I didn't understand most of it. But now, as an adult, I know it is a wonderful story, very similar to my life experiences.

Mrs. Peterson, my fourth-grade teacher, shared my love of reading. Every afternoon we all sat quietly at our desks as she read one of her favorite books to us, the same books every year, year after year, books like *My Friend Flicka*, *Lassie Come Home*, or *Lad: A Dog*. She would get emotional when she got to the sad parts and would have to turn the reading over to me because she was crying so hard we couldn't understand her.

In high school one of my favorite after-school activities was to go to the used bookstore downtown and search the shelves for the oldest books or books from my favorite writers, such as Sinclair Lewis.

English Literature was always my favorite class, and I never minded having to write essays, poetry, or short stories.

My love of reading and writing never left me, but life got in the way. I was studying to be a social worker in college and wanted to save the world. Instead I had four children and became a businesswoman, the founder and president of a sports marketing and management company. Over the years, I occasionally kept a few things I had written; letters, newspaper clippings, and pictures and stuck them away somewhere.

I always thought someday I would write a book about my life, the things I've learned, the things I wanted to share with my children, the things I wanted to share with other women. And as I got closer to retirement, I decided I better get going on the book. I asked my daughters to pull out anything in the warehouse that might be of value to my writing plans. I didn't expect much, but a couple weeks later, my middle daughter, Ellen, showed up with seventeen file boxes with everything I had saved. Going through the boxes has proven to be a never-ending task and the source for this memoir. It has been a bigger endeavor than I'd ever dreamed and a tremendous amount of work. Sometimes I sit down at my computer thinking I'm going to spend just thirty minutes writing this morning, and before I know it, it's afternoon. And while it's been a laborious task, it has also a been a joy that I will never regret.

Table of Contents

One

The disintegration of my marriage probably played a major role in how I became one of a handful of women who were directors of major marathons in the United States at that time.

In 1984 my troubled twenty-four-year marriage became an impossible situation. It reached a boiling point on September 10, 1984, when my husband came home from the office in an obviously foul mood.

He refused dinner, poured a glass of wine, and went into the den to watch TV. Our twenty-year-old son, Patrick, had recently moved out to live with two of his buddies. He and his friend, Chris, stopped by that evening to dry their laundry, and we were all sitting, talking quietly in the kitchen. All of a sudden, my husband stormed out of the den, grabbed our son, and pushed him up against the wall.

Patrick knew from experience that this could turn explosive and that he needed to get out of the house. He tried to leave, but my husband had him cornered in the kitchen and continued to push and slap him and call him names and challenge him to fight.

Somehow Patrick was able to get to the door and was trying to get in his truck and get away, but my husband grabbed a chain from the garage and began pounding on the truck, trying to break the window to get at my son. At that point, my husband's anger turned on us, my daughter Christine and I. He pushed and choked me and kicked fourteen-year-old Christine in her ribs and threatened both of us. "Don't ever tell me what to do in my own home" he said before pouring another drink and retreating to the den. I called the police. This was not the first time he had blown up like this. He had attacked Patrick once before, when he had him down on the floor trying to strangle him. It took the girls and I to stop him and pull him off. On several occasions, he had slapped neighborhood children because they were in our yard or making too much noise.

Road rage was common with him. If he felt another driver got in his way, he was apt to chase him and run him off the road, and if he could get him to get out of his car, all the better, because he was always ready to fight, even if the kids and I were in the car, terrified. Several times neighbors called the police because of his behavior, but this night was the first time I had called for help.

The police responded within a few minutes. My husband was belligerent when they asked him what was going on. "It's none of your business" was his response. He was getting more and more agitated, and when he raised a fist to hit one of them, they called for backup. It took four officers to subdue him and to get him in handcuffs. He kept calling to me for help, shouting "Lynn, help me! They are hurting me."

The responding officers were calm and kind. They searched the house for weapons and then assured me "don't worry, you're safe. He will be held for at least seventy-two hours and you'll be notified when he's released."

They were wrong. He was released within a few hours, walked the eight miles home barefoot, and climbed through a window to

2

get back into our house. When we heard the commotion, I quickly gathered the girls and tried to get them together in one bedroom. When Ellen heard her father come through the window, she was terrified. She ran out the front door and down the street with me in hot pursuit. I dragged her, kicking and screaming, trying to con-sole her and convince her that everything would be all right if we all stayed together.

We barricaded ourselves in one bedroom until we were sure he was sleeping soundly. We could hear him snoring in the bedroom down the hall, as though nothing had ever happened that night. My oldest daughter, Katie, spent the night sitting on the floor with her back pressed against the bedroom door, determined she would not let her father in.

As soon as it was light, I borrowed clothes and shoes from my daughters so I could go on with my day. I dropped Christine and Ellen off at their high school, reminding them, "Remember, this is family business and we don't talk about it to anyone."

I realize now how wrong it was to keep them from telling some-one, talking to a counselor, or at least to their best friends.

And then I went on to a meeting with new clients about an event they wanted me to do. I pulled into my clients' parking lot early and sat in my car in a daze.

Do I look okay? I wondered. Will they notice anything? Can I handle this meeting? What just happened? An elderly couple walked by my car, hand in hand. That will never be me, I thought. Now the tears began. I rarely share this story with anyone, but it's still so real to me, it seems like yesterday.

The kids and I were sheltered that first night by Katie's boyfriend, Steve, and his three roommates in their little apartment in Pacific Beach. Still shaking and unable to sleep, I sat on the floor playing Scrabble till dawn with Charlie, one of Steve's roommates. The next day a good friend, one of my running friends, Officer Gary Reichley, spotted our police report when he got to the station, and immediately contacted me. He and his wife, a US Marshall, insisted that the kids and I come and stay with them until things settled down. They also encouraged me to meet with someone from the YWCA who dealt with abused women. I was not ready to consider myself abused. That came later.

I picked the girls up after school every day, and we would very cautiously go back to our house, making sure he wasn't there, then go in to get clean clothes and clean up any dirty dishes he had left for me.

After a couple weeks, my husband's parents persuaded him to move in with them. Once he moved, I felt it was safe for the kids and I to move back into our home.

We were in family counseling for a year, sometimes individually and sometimes he and I together, and on rare occasions, he met with the children. When the year of therapy was up, the therapist advised me: "It's time for you to move on. You can't change him; you can't fix him; you have to take care of yourself and your chil-dren. You need to file for a divorce."

She gave me the name and phone number of a divorce attor-ney. I kept the card in my pocket for several weeks. Having grown up in a strong Catholic family, divorce was a difficult decision, but with a measure of sadness, I finally took her advice and hired the attorney she had recommended.

The attorney began our first session by explaining the law to me - what I was entitled to after a twenty-four-year marriage. I stopped her and said, "I don't want anything. I just want a safe and peaceful environment for my children and myself."

She thought I was foolish, even stupid, and she continued to tell me what I should get from the divorce.

"He has a good job and much better job opportunities than you. You should get alimony and part or even half of his retire-ment." I think she thought my life was over. I refused to

4

listen. I finally agreed that I would at least accept the minimum child sup-port required by law for Ellen and Christine until they finished high school.

I was responsible for taking care of the house. I managed the yard, cut the grass, trimmed the trees, planted the gardens, and even lugged railroad ties home and used them to build retaining walls in our backyard.

I also did all the painting and wallpapering. But to be fair, he did start painting the eaves on one side of the house. It took him over two years to finish one small section. I finally took that job over and painted the whole house inside and out.

Did I mention trees? My kids and I dug deep holes on the bank behind our house and we planted big pine trees. The last time I drove by that house, those pine trees had turned into a forest.

I'll give him credit, he managed the finances. I was allowed to use the checkbook to go grocery shopping once a week, and I had to be sure to bring him the receipt.

It takes two people to make a good marriage, but it also takes two people to make a bad marriage, and I have to take responsibility for my share. I think I was way too young to get married and maybe too stubborn.

I didn't tell anyone for several months about the end of my marriage, not even my family and certainly not my friends. Because my brothers and my sister and I all contributed to my parents' rent, I realized I wouldn't be able to do this anymore, so I eventually had to tell my siblings. They immediately surrounded me with their love and understanding. They insisted we had to tell my parents.

Although I had no steady income, no credit cards, and I didn't even have my own checking account, my mind was made up: I will make it on my own! I will survive!

Two

My First Event

I was born in Detroit, Michigan, but my only important memory of Detroit is of hiding under my bed for fear of being punished for something I had done. I don't remember what I did, but I do clearly remember the fuss I created by hiding for hours under my bed while my parents searched frantically for me. Then the neighbors and finally the police joined the search. No one thought to look under my bed, but I eventually came out because it was dinner time and I was hungry.

We left the big city when I was four and moved north to Hubbard Lake, one of the largest inland lakes in Michigan. Six miles long and two miles across, it is located in a beautiful, wooded, remote area in the northern part of the Lower Peninsula of Michigan.

My parents were very young when they made that move, and they had never lived in the country. They bought a small, rundown summer resort twenty miles from the nearest store and thirty miles from the nearest school. My dad bought a hammer and learned to repair the cabins, and then he bought a how-to book and learned how to build cabins. Our second winter there, we were snowed in for six weeks, which meant no school, no electricity, and no running water. Once a week, a small plane dropped food and mail on the frozen lake for the few families who braved the winter.

My older brother, John, and I rode the school bus every day, leaving home early in the morning and returning home late in the afternoon. For much of the school year we left home before dawn and got home after dark.

There were no other children living year-round in Hubbard Lake, but I had a friend in the summertime. Her name was Lois, and she was the same age as I was. I was delighted to have a friend, but soon I realized she wasn't really a good friend. She was mean to me. One day she told me to go in the outhouse to look for something. I did as she told me, and she locked me in there for a long time, maybe hours or maybe ten minutes. Whatever it was, I was really scared.

Another time we were playing catch in her bedroom and she threw the ball and broke the window. Her mother came running upstairs to see what had happened, and Lois told her I had broken

Lynn and Lois

the window. Her mother accepted this story, and I was too shy to argue. That relationship really impacted me. I felt so inferior to Lois, and her mother made it worse when she told me I had dirty fingernails.

After a few more years of isolation, my parents sold the resort and we moved to what seemed like a big city - Harrisville. It had 450 people, three churches, three bars, a bowling alley, and a small, brick two-story school that housed kindergarten through twelfth grade.

I have always considered Harrisville my hometown. It was a sleepy little town in northern Michigan, on Lake Huron, a town with only one stoplight, and a telephone operator who always knew everything about everybody.

I liked it, but it wasn't perfect. When I was eleven, I decided that this little town was too boring. It needed something new, something different. After thinking carefully, for about ten minutes, I decided a cat show would be great! I had never had a cat nor did I even like cats, but I didn't let that deter me. I started right away gathering all the cats I could find. It wasn't easy getting them to come home with me. It took quite a few scratches, but I got them there one by one and put them in our basement. Then I made some quick signs promoting my show and put them up all over Harrisville.

After sufficiently notifying everyone in town, I came home to check on the cats and was headed back out to find a few more candidates for my show. Suddenly my Dad walked in the front door. He was now the Ford dealer in town, and he had spotted one of the signs in front of his dealership, had come home immediately, and made me release all the cats. I can still hear him shout, "Get those damn cats out of our house—now!" That was the end of my first event.

John, my older brother and Mark, my middle brother and I, shared a big bedroom with a window that overlooked the only two-lane highway in that part of the state. There was a Sunoco gas station across the street, and we were quite certain that some night it was going to be robbed, so we set up a schedule and took turns keeping watch for the bad guys. Each of us would take our two-hour turn sitting at the window and waiting patiently. The bad guys never came.

When I was thirteen, I convinced the owner of a vacant store on Main Street to let me hold a dance in his empty storefront. I convinced my brother, John, to help me because he had a record player, and we shared a couple records. Once again, I made signs and posted them around town and all the kids in Harrisville, all twenty of them, came to the dance. We served punch and played Bill Haley's "Rock around the Clock" over and over until 9:00 p.m. The dance was a big success. Although I didn't recognize it then, I seemed to be headed for a career in event management.

When I was fifteen, I heard about a private girls' boarding school and decided I wanted to go there. St. Mary's Academy was three hundred miles from home, in Monroe, Michigan, just across the state line from Ohio. I was bored and convinced that I needed to go to a better school that offered more interesting classes. Dad was very much opposed to the idea - he wanted all of us to stay close to home forever, but my mother encouraged both John and I to consider better schools than those offered in Harrisville.

Both John and I won our battles. He went to Catholic Central in Alpena, thirty miles to the north, and I went to St. Mary's Academy, in Monroe, Michigan.

I was terribly homesick for the first couple of weeks of school, but then I settled into the rigid routine of 6:00 a.m. mass, then breakfast, followed by classes including English, History, Latin, Science, Geography, Religion, Drama, and even piano lessons. The campus was beautiful, with acres of fruit trees, a small lake, and rolling hills of farmland. We wore uniforms all day, prayed together before and after meals, and maintained total silence from 7:00 p.m. to 7:00 a.m.

I shared a room with Barbara from Flint, Michigan, and Joanne from Los Angeles. We became fast friends and spent any of our free time together. But that all changed when the nuns asked me to move to another room with just one other student. Linda, my new roommate, was having a difficult time adapting and was dis-liked by most of the other students. The nuns decided I would be a good companion for Linda. She was a challenge, but within a few weeks we were friends, and gradually the other students began to treat her as an equal.

The day I came home at the end of my first year at St. Mary's, my parents announced that we were moving to San Diego, California, the next week, which was a complete surprise to my brothers and I. My sister, Mary Denise, was a baby then, so she didn't care.

I was excited about seeing California, meeting new friends and new cousins, and seeing movie stars everywhere. The excitement wore off two weeks after we arrived in San Diego, when I started school.

My first day at Hoover High School was September 1956. It was horrible that first day, and it didn't get much better. Only two or three of the three thousand students even spoke to me for the first few weeks. I think it was because I dressed differently than everyone else. I wore saddle shoes and bobby socks, which I learned were very "old school" in San Diego. All the other girls wore flats at that time and no socks.

My cousin, Pamela Jansen, was born and raised in San

Diego. I had met her only once when her family had visited us in Michigan. She was also a student at Hoover High School, but she was two years older than me. I passed her every day in the hall, but she always acted as though she didn't know me. She would turn her head and laugh and whisper to her friends as they all had lunch together at their special table in the cafeteria. I sat across the room, alone and miserable, pretending I was just fine.

The move to San Diego was the first of many moves. We moved and I changed high schools six times during my high school years. My Dad was always looking for a better life for the whole family.

These frequent moves created insecurity and loneliness—there was seldom time to make friends. Classes were never the same, but somehow I managed to learn a few things and get decent grades. I might start with a Spanish class in September and have to switch to a Latin class in November and back to Spanish two months later as I changed schools again.

Growing up in a very small town, I had known everyone and had lots of friends. Suddenly I knew almost no one and had zero friends. Each move got a little easier, or maybe I just got used to it. Fortunately, I spent my senior year at only one school, Cathedral Girls High School, in downtown San Diego. I really liked it and settled in quickly.

I worked hard in my senior year, got good grades, made some great lifelong friends including my wonderful sister-in-law, Pat McElhaney who later married my brother, John.

I was beginning to plan for college. My dream was to go to the University of San Diego. I knew very little about my parents' financial situation except that it was constantly fluctuating. We were seen as the richest family in Harrisville when we lived there, but that all changed once we started moving and my Dad was frequently changing jobs. I still remember having beautiful, expensive lamps in our living room but no money to buy light bulbs.

There was never a conversation about how or where I would go to college or where the money would come from. I just made up my mind that I would go to USD, so I applied and was accepted. I also applied for a summer job in the school library,

READY FOR NEW SCHOOL YEAR—Norma Peck, left, former student body president at Academy of Our Lady of Peace; Barbara Breveleri, last year's senior class president at Rosary High School, and Lynn Coseo of Cathedral Girls' High, who has made the highest score in the placement tests given this year, make an early visit to the College for Women in anticipation of the start of their college careers on the Alcala Park campus.

Lynn (far right) as a USD Freshmen

and I got that too. Every dollar I made in the library went toward my tuition. At that rate it would have taken me twenty years to pay off my full tuition. But that didn't matter. I loved everything about it: the atmosphere of the university, the classes I would be taking, and all those books in the library surrounding me.

Toward the end of the summer, the director of the library told me to dress up the next day because they were going to take my picture. There was no explanation for the change in dress or for the picture, but I followed directions and wore my best and only dress to work. There were two other girls there for the picture taking, and they were each introduced to me as the student body president of their respective high schools. I was impressed. Here I was, a nobody. I didn't get it.

A week later our pictures appeared in the newspaper, mine with the caption "USD Freshman Who Scored Highest on the Entrance Exam." That was me! I was called into the president's office and told that I had won a full academic scholarship because of my score which explained the picture.

Freshman year started, and about that same time I met my first serious boyfriend, Pat Flanagan. Pat was also starting his freshman year in college after a four-year stint in the Air Force. We were both from the Midwest and yearned to be back there; me to Michigan and Pat to Wisconsin.

Neither of us had adapted very well to the Southern California lifestyle. We dated exclusively through our freshman and sophomore years before deciding to get married.

As usual, I made major decisions without listening to my parents or to any other adults. When I told my counselor at the university of my plans, she was upset. "You're making a big mistake, and your scholarship will not be renewed if you do this" was her response to me. As usual, I stood my ground and said, "Thank you, but I'm getting married anyway."

A Life in Motion

I was twenty years old and thought I knew everything.

Pat and I decided that he would go to school full-time and I would work to support both of us. I got a job in the corporate trust department of a downtown bank and started to work full-time.

I soon realized I didn't want to give up my education, so after my eight-hour workdays at the bank ended, I hopped on a bus and got to USD in time to work in the dining hall, waiting on other students and picking up their dirty dishes for two hours before my evening class, which ended at 10:00 p.m. I also worked all day Saturdays doing odd jobs on campus such as polishing sterling silver.

Pat and I got married in June after my sophomore year in a traditional Catholic wedding. A year later we made another major decision - again, not a very smart one. We packed our meager belongings and moved to Stevens Point, Wisconsin, where Pat wanted to finish his education and become a park ranger in the wilderness.

We rented an old house on Main Street with a an elderly woman living upstairs. She controlled the thermostat, and we paid the bill. She liked it really warm. It was a small town; everyone was friendly and eager to tell us all about Ed Gein, the local mass murderer who had made lampshades out of his victims' skin.

There were few jobs available in this small town and no night classes. I was seven months pregnant at that point, so Pat ended up working and not going to school. His parents were still in San Diego. They encouraged us to return to San Diego and offered to pay his tuition if he completed his education at USD. We ended up returning to San Diego with one-year-old Katie and another baby on the way.

Three

HOW IT ALL BEGAN

My husband had earned his degree in accounting and was working as the CFO for a small manufacturing company, but he was not happy. Accounting was not for him. He still wanted to be a park ranger in the wilderness. He found parenting four busy children a challenge, but it was a joy for me.

I had joined Las Amigas, a fundraising branch of the Children's Home Society and became president of the club after one year. I also started a neighborhood playgroup that functioned almost like a preschool with art projects, story hour, and of course snacks. I recruited five other mothers to join in so that no one had to run the program more than once a week.

When Katie was four she started having severe seizures. After her second seizure, I took her to see a neurologist. He wasn't very friendly - just very matter-of-fact. "Your child has a serious condition. We need to get her in the hospital right away for some tests." I tried hard not to cry in front of Katie, but she quizzed me all the way home. She always called me Honey Mama, and this day was no exception.

"What's wrong, Honey Mama? Are you sad, Honey Mama?" came the little voice from the backseat.

The tests were completed and confirmed that she had an abnormality in a group of vessels in the left side of her brain, which was causing the seizures. She was diagnosed with epilepsy.

The doctor very matter-of-factly told me that she might get better once she reached puberty, or she could get worse. She was on medication for the next twelve years and had brain scans once a year. The fear of the unknown never left my mind. I needed to help my child so I got involved in the epilepsy organization, served on the board of directors, and helped form the Epilepsy Society, a fund-raising organization that is still active today, more than fifty years later.

The doctor was right. When she was sixteen, her annual tests showed that the abnormality had corrected itself, and she never had another seizure.

My children always played well and worked well together so it was natural for them to start a business when they were very young: the Flanagan Cookie Company. They took orders on Friday and loaded up their red wagon to deliver fresh cookies on Saturday— several choices including chocolate chip, peanut butter, oatmeal, and snickerdoodle. It was great for them, but it was costing me more than if they bought the cookies at the store, and my kitchen was a mess.

Eventually they switched from cookies to macrame. They made enough money crafting plant hangers for all of us to go to Hawaii for two weeks. They were already becoming hardworking, knowledgeable businesspeople, and they were still kids.

• • •

My husband was forty-two and I was thirty-seven, and we weren't getting any younger. Our fifteen-year-old son had been having discipline problems at school and also in the neighborhood. It was getting worse. I took him to see a therapist, and after a couple of sessions, the therapist said all the tests indicated that I was a single parent; that my son had no father. By this time, I had to face it and admit to myself what a mistake I had made in getting married so young and walking away from my scholarship so easily.

My husband started seeing a psychiatrist, who was quite certain that there was nothing wrong with him. "He drinks a lot, but he isn't an alcoholic. He doesn't drink during the day, only at night when he comes home. You two just need to talk more." Obviously this psychiatrist didn't know much about alcoholism. Just because he only drank after 5 o'clock, he was still an alcoholic whose drinking was playing havoc with his family.

I was determined to make my marriage work and to finish raising my children. I had gone back to school, completed the medical assisting program at a community college, got a certificate in radiology, and went to work for a group of urologists.

My husband, in the meantime, was just not happy with life in general. His behavior towards me and our children clearly reflected his attitude. I accepted responsibility and struggled to make him happy. He didn't like having dinner with the kids, so I made sure I fed them before he got home and that they were quiet when we heard him come through the front door. He would walk through the house turning off every light he felt was unnecessary. Then he would pull a bottle of scotch out of the cupboard and settle down in front of the TV. Sometimes I tried hiding the scotch before he got home, but that only made it worse. He always found it, and when he did, he took it out on me.

17

I knew he liked volleyball so I researched to find him a class that he would really enjoy. I was right! He loved the program that I found for him. He liked his teammates and even liked the mile they ran before they played volleyball, which I thought was strange. How could anyone run a whole mile?

Shortly after he started the volleyball program, I found a children's running program and registered my two youngest daughters, Ellen and Christine. They loved running and were very competitive. I drove them to their sessions twice a week and sat in the car reading a book until they were finished. After their second week in the class, I decided that instead of waiting in the car for them, I might as well put the time to good use and tried running myself. By third week, I was hooked.

I was running nearly every day and loving it. This was in 1981. At that time, I was working for a young urologist who had just started his practice and was eager to get new patients. He knew that I had started running and thought that might be a good way to attract some patients. He offered to pay the entry fees for my daughter, Katie and I to run in a 5K race at Mission Bay. He also paid for our shirts and had them printed across the back with the catchy phrase C ME 2 P. Our shirts got a lot of attention, but I'm not sure he got any new clients from it. That first run was the beginning of my lifelong love affair with running that has lasted for over forty-five year, much longer than my first marriage.

Not long after that race a neighbor and friend who was a fundraiser for the American Red Cross asked me to help her put together a race to raise money for her organization. I jumped at the chance, thinking that I must know something about putting on a race. How hard could it be?

I quickly realized that I knew just about nothing, but I learned. I enrolled my neighbors, friends, and relatives to help. The kids enrolled their friends and to ensure that they would show up on time, we invited all of them to spend the night before the race at our house. We called it Extend Yourself 15K because all the races at that time were either a 5K or a 10K and I wanted to be different. It was surprisingly successful with fifteen hundred happy runners.

The very next day after Extend Yourself, the owner of a running store in Ocean Beach tracked me down, called me, and asked if I would put on a race for them. This second event was the Ocean Beach 10K. Within a few months I was very busy and started to get too many phone calls at work, so I decided to quit my job taking X-rays and looking for kidney stones. I would just put on road races!

Lynn running a race at Torrey Pines State Beach

Four

GAME ON

By 1985 my divorce was over. My ex-husband wanted me to sell our home and give him half of the equity. He let me have theother half to buy a home for myself and my children. My plan was to work hard to make enough money to support my children until they finished school. Then maybe I would go in the convent. The latter part of that plan didn't last long.

I now had over a dozen events and had outgrown my little office, which was a corner of my kitchen counter. I had a phone, a portable typewriter, and a cardboard filing case. My son Patrick had moved out with several buddies, so I took advantage of the empty space and moved my office into his bedroom.

My work level had increased, but so had my running mileage. I was now averaging at least forty miles a week and was getting ready to run my first marathon. Running was not as popular with women in the 1980s as it is now. In fact, there were only two types of running shoes for women: a Nike and a Reebok, both leather, heavy, and stiff.
There was also very little information for women about training, nutrition, or gear. I got up early on marathon morning,

ate a huge breakfast because I knew I wouldn't eat again for a while, and then tied on my brand new running shoes. By mile fifteen I was sure I was going to die. Everything hurt and that breakfast I ate? Not a good idea. I made it to the finish line and then collapsed on the ground.

My youngest daughter, Christine, was huddled over me crying, "Mommy, are you going to die?" My response was, "Oh, I hope so."

The paramedics got me moving again, but I swore I would never ever run again. I was going to burn my running shoes as soon as I got home.

Two days later I was in Philippides Running Store trying on new running shoes and looking for information on coaches. I got the shoes and hooked up with a great coach, Ted Van Arsdale. Three months later I ran the Mission Bay Marathon, much faster and now convinced that I could do anything I set out to do.

The first time a client, the regional marketing director for Buick, came to my home for a meeting, I realized I probably needed a real office. Now I had to get serious about finding some office space or maybe buying a running shoe store, my other dream. I had no money to buy or start a shoe store, but maybe I could find a cheap office. About that time, my good running friend, Gary Reichley, a San Diego police officer, had approached me about handling their Copper Bowl 10K, an annual race between the police depart-ment and the sheriff's department. Part of the proposal included six months usage of a one-room office with three desks. I jumped at the chance.

When the event was over and the six month lease was up, I quickly found new office space: a two-bedroom house in a residential neighborhood very close to home. It worked well because it had a garage and a kitchen and a bathroom and even space for three or four volunteers, who worked every day for a few hours.

Our stay there was short, however, because the landlord, who knew exactly what I planned to do with the space, failed to mention that absolutely no businesses were allowed in this quiet residential area. I should have known more about zoning, but I was still new to most aspects of business.

It was a short time before big trucks started unloading boxes of T-shirts, entry forms, and bib numbers, while volunteers started arriving to stuff envelopes. The longtime residents were fast to start filing complaints with the city. They won., we lost and were forced to start packing.

Once again, I got lucky. One of my new clients was growing and needed to move to a bigger space, but he first needed to break his current lease. Their space was perfect for me - more room, beautiful location in Crown Point, and plenty of places to run, which was important to me. I felt like I had a real business now. I set up a bank account, hired several part-time people, got a couple electric typewriters, and decided on a name for my business.

In Motion was born and I learned how much I didn't know about business. I read books and business magazines and talked to my very successful brothers, John Coseo and Chris Coseo. I learned. I learned how to prepare budgets, how to get permits, how to write contracts, how to prepare and distribute press releases, how to prepare sponsorship proposals and actually sell sponsorship, how to recruit volunteers and elite athletes, and how to market to the masses. I learned to plan breakfast meetings, luncheons, and major receptions.

I also realized that my ten-to-twelve-hour workdays were not enough. I needed more help.

I was starting to meet lots of people in the running community. One in particular told me he really admired the work I was doing, and he wanted to help me. He was bright, aggressive, and had a penchant for road racing. He'd worked in marketing for some big companies and also owned a small business himself, and best of all, he was willing to work part-time for very little money. I quickly hired him.

We worked well together for a few years, but gradually we both agreed that our standards were quite different. He was enthralled with the elite athletes, those few athletes who are paid to run, the athletes who won our races. I didn't mind paying the winner's prize money, but I believed that the last place finisher was just as important as the first place, and that's how I insisted we treat every participant in our events. He was also adept at exaggerating, and I wasn't good at it.

Because he had a background in running a business and I didn't, I let him oversee the financial end of the business. My loyal bookkeeper pulled me aside one day and said, "You better start looking at the books, or you're going to lose this company."

She was right. I am still grateful to Linda! I couldn't believe how much money we owed. I insisted that he and I sit down and go over the books together immediately. He agreed that we were in trouble. His suggestion was that we close the company and walk away from any debt we had, but I refused to do that. Because I had created In Motion and I owned majority stock, I wasn't about to give it up, and I certainly wouldn't walk away from the debt and leave our vendors hanging. With a lot of hard work, I managed to keep things running and gradually paid off the debt.

I wanted to be fair, so I gave him several of our events, including the Carlsbad 5000. He also wanted to keep his company car, but since it was in my name and he didn't have insurance, but he did have a glove box stuffed with unpaid parking tickets, I had to say no to keeping the car.

That caused a rift between us that lasted for many years.

True to his word, he walked away from the debt, started a new company, brought in investors, and eventually sold the company for millions of dollars.

My clients at that time included Jack in the Box, Southwest Airlines, Alaska Airlines, Albertsons, Vons, Toyota, BMW, Glendale Federal, and a number of others. Very soon In Motion was producing events every weekend with a staff of four-to-five full-time people. Calls were coming in almost daily from someone who wanted us to put on an event for a nonprofit or better yet, from a company who wanted to sponsor one of our events. The most exciting call, out of the blue, came from the Heart of San Diego Marathon, the very marathon I had just participated in. Their board had decided that they couldn't depend entirely on volunteers to produce such an important event and that they needed a professional, and that was me. I was ecstatic! With this 1985 Heart of San Diego Marathon contract, I became one of a handful of female directors of major marathons in the country.

Lynn with Frank Shorter

Five

A WOMAN SURVIVING IN A MAN'S WORLD

I was definitely a woman stepping into a man's world. It was interesting, but I had to fight to hold my own, which I did. So many times, in a meeting with all men, I had to force my way into a conversation to assure them that I knew what I was doing and that I was in charge.

The other aspect of being in my position was that there could be unwelcome advances and propositions thrown at me. While most of my male clients were gentlemen and treated me with respect, there were others who definitely were not.

There were those who offered to help me in getting right to the top of our industry and told me what they had done for other women and what they could do for me if I cooperated. I pretended I didn't know what they were talking about. There were men who embarrassed me with their crude remarks, which they thought were funny. I didn't laugh.

There were men who invited me to join them for a weekend in Las Vegas or on an extravagant boating trip, and these propositions usually came from married men. I learned how to reject their offers and invitations quickly and firmly while still managing to maintain the necessary professional relationship.

It was a very different time then when men could get away with this. Women ignored it because we had no choice.

"A woman in a man's world"

I had no interest in ever getting married again or even dating. I had had enough, but between my work and running, I was constantly surrounded by men. If they expressed any interest, usually I was too busy to even notice it.

I often ran with men because I was fast and competitive. I usually finished in the top three or four of my age group in races, and I liked the challenge of running with men. I even got to run with the well-known B Team, a group of San Diego's fastest male runners at that time. One afternoon they had gathered for a ten-mile run around Mission Bay, and they challenged me to

26

stay with them for the first mile. I accepted the challenge, which turned out to be a relaxed 6:30 mile pace for them and a fastest-ever mile for me. I stayed with them, side by side for the whole mile but was glad to say goodbye as they took off for the rest of the run.

One day I got a call from a law enforcement officer who just wanted to express his appreciation for the races that I had produced. He was a fan and ran in all my events. He then asked if I would consider running with him sometime.

He sounded nice and harmless, so I agreed to go for a run with him the next week. He came to my office, and as we started our run, he seemed uneasy. Something about him just didn't seem right. I didn't feel comfortable, so I ran with him once but never again. I managed to be in a meeting or out of the office whenever he called after that.

He started to watch me at races, leaving me messages and writing letters to tell me how much he respected and admired me. I stopped taking his calls and stuck his letters in my desk drawer just in case I ever needed them. But he still continued to follow me at races. My staff kept an eye on him and made sure he never got too close.

A few months after our run, a young woman was murdered by a highway patrolman who pulled her over on the freeway late one night. The next day I received a message from the man who was following me, telling me not to be afraid. The officer who murdered the woman on the freeway was his partner, but he knew nothing about what had happened. He insisted that I never tell anyone that I even knew him. It sounded almost like a threat. It scared me.

I decided to call my good friend, Gary Reichley, from the San Diego Police Department and told him what was going on. He reassured me, but he sounded concerned. Twenty minutes later he and three detectives were in my office. They took the cards and letters that the stalker had sent me, put a tap on my phone, and began an investigation of him. They later learned that I was not the first woman this guy had stalked, and that he had been transferred out of the area, but he never tried to contact me again.

Six

Battles Lost and Battles Won

Just like life, business isn't always easy. There are usually at least a few bumps along the road. Right after I signed my contract with the American Heart Association to direct their eighth annual event, I discovered not just a bump, but a mountain.

As I usually do, I started working on the project by securing all the necessary permits. I was shocked when my permit request to the US Navy was promptly denied with the following letter:

Dear Ms. Flanagan,

In response to your letter of June 26, 1985, requesting permission to use Naval Air Station North Island for your annual Heart of San Diego Marathon, I am sorry to inform you that your request has been denied.

As we briefed the race committee last year, due to new security guidelines we can no longer open our gates to such large crowds as you require. Crowds of eight to ten thousand people place a very large and unknown strain not only on security but on manpower in daily operations as well. I'm sorry we cannot help you in this manner.

This came from the commanding officer, Department of the Navy, Naval Air Station, North Island. This looked official, but I wasn't giving up. I contacted my congressman, Duncan Hunter, who agreed to help by pleading our case with North Island Airbase. The result? A much longer and more detailed rejection letter. The navy's response was followed closely by a rejection from the City of Coronado, the home of the naval air base. If the US Navy wasn't going to play, the City of Coronado certainly wasn't going to play either. We had hit a brick wall - one I certainly didn't see coming.

Here we were, less than five months from race day, and we had no starting line. How could we establish a finish line without a start-ing line? I had work to do! I began by finding a new starting line. After I had considered every possible location, the light bulb went on in my head: the tidelands at the foot of the Coronado Bay Bridge! It was acres of parkland, there was plenty of parking, and it would have little negative impact on nearby residents. It would just require picking up a few more miles in San Diego, and I was confident we could do that. It would work without the Navy, but first we had to turn the "N0" from Coronado officials to an "AYE AYE!

The next step was to recruit supporters from Coronado as well as San Diego; city officials, retired military officers, business own-ers, athletes, and of course, the media. I wanted as many support-ers as possible at the upcoming September 3, 1985, Coronado City Council meeting. It worked. We packed the house. I explained the value of the event to the community and how the benefits far out-weighed any possible negatives. We answered any questions from the council or the audience. The council said yes, and the crowd cheered. We were on our way.

The new course worked like a charm and as a result of

our work, other nonprofit organizations were allowed to use our course for their future events. We had climbed that mountain, but it wasn't the last.

As a runner, I was always looking for good places to run or walk - different areas, fun, scenic, safe, places. We had worked with Caltrans on a number of projects and found them to be a challenging, but fair organization to work with. In a meeting for another event my Caltrans contact, San Diego County Director John McAllister, was sitting next to me. Already anticipating his answer, I lightheartedly asked him when we could run a race on Highway 163, the beautiful tree-shaded roadway through Balboa Park. Of course he said, "Never."

Over the years, whenever I ran into John at a meeting, I brought up the topic of closing 163 for an event. He always laughed and changed the subject. Then one day he called to tell me that he was retiring next year and that he had one thing he wanted to complete before his last day. He wanted to issue a permit to In Motion to close down a portion of 163 for a race.

"You better start working on your application and also be at my retirement party."

I was speechless. It had been ten years, but I hadn't given up. And I had the perfect client for that first run down the freeway: the *San Diego Union Tribune.* We had been working with the newspaper on the Race for Literacy for several years. It was a popular event that ran around Balboa Park and down Sixth Avenue to downtown San Diego.

With the closure of the freeway, we were able to put our superstar, the Cat in the Hat, in the pace car leading thousands of runners and walkers down the freeway on foot. Together with the newspaper, Caltrans, and the Cat, we were able to attract many more runners, while raising hundreds of thousands

31

Lynn's grandchildren, Caleb and Hannah with the Cat in Hat

of dollars over the years to help raise the level of literacy in our community. I also had the pleasure of getting to know Audrey Geisel, the Cat's real mother.

• • •

A Life in Motion

Producing a marathon in San Diego has never been an easy task for a number of reasons namely the geography. San Diego is a beautiful city, but Interstate 5 and busy railroad tracks make it difficult to get runners to the ocean. In Motion had the good fortune of putting several miles of the Heart of San Diego Marathon course on the ocean-front boardwalk one year. The Toyotas leading the runners had to drop out for the boardwalk section because their weight could potentially cause the boardwalk to cave in, or high surf could be a danger to the participants; it could mean more than just getting wet. Police officers on motorcycles led the way that year, but after that it was decided that the boardwalk was off-limits to cars and even to police on motorcycles.

So our wonderful course was short-lived. We got right to work again on Monday brainstorming a new course. There had to be something that the city would bless so that we could have a course we knew the runners would like. Finally came a middle-of-the-night-can't-sleep idea. Why not keep it all on the coast? Run from Torrey Pines to Oceanside?

After several years of struggling to design a really great course, we realized this might work. I had met with the City Special Events Department to propose a variety of different courses, but there was always a reason to shoot it down: maybe a neighborhood who didn't like runners, a church on the course that had a service at the same time as the race, or not enough manpower to oversee all the traffic. They were all valid reasons (I guess). So here went another meeting.

I told the San Diego decision makers what we wanted to do. We were now fewer than three months from race day, and they were probably as tired of seeing me as I was of them so they finally gave in.

"Do it your way this year, and then as soon as the race is

over, let's sit down and come up with a better course here within the San Diego city limits. We don't want you to leave permanently. We will supply the officers needed for our part of the course this year."

We immediately got to work on getting the permits for the upcoming San Diego Marathon, now only two months away. I met with the decision makers from Oceanside, Carlsbad, Leucadia, Encinitas, Solana Beach, and Del Mar. We started at the top and headed south and it was going well. That's where we hit a bump. Del Mar definitely did not want marathoners running through their quiet, "pristine" village and were clearly voicing their opposition. I got on the phone and called each of the Del Mar City Council members to plead my case. Their responses were varied. Some said "maybe" and some said "absolutely not." There were no resounding yeses. I wasn't feeling very good about the upcoming city council meeting, where the decision would be made.

I just had to keep fighting. Mike Aguirre, former San Diego City Attorney, community activist, and a runner, called to give me some advice. He suggested I use my media contacts and stage a press conference on the southern border of Del Mar at five o'clock the day before the council meeting. We did that and got a good turnout - all the media were there, but I still didn't feel very confident.

The Oscar Mayer Wienermobile was in town, heard the story, and wanted to help, so they came to city hall just before the council meeting started and passed out hot dogs. The supporters wagged hot dogs at the Del Mar City Council members as they entered the meeting. It was on all the evening news that night. The crowd loved it, but the council didn't. They simply did not want to disturb their citizens on a quiet Sunday morning, even though it would take the marathoners only thirty to forty-five minutes to clear the Del Mar section of the race.

Now we were only two months out; people were registering, coming from all over the country, but we couldn't tell them where the marathon would be.

On Monday we redesigned the course to move the whole event to Oceanside and Carlsbad with the start and finish at the pier in Oceanside. I was able to get in to see both the city manager of Oceanside and the city manager of Carlsbad, Ray Patchette, on Monday. They both liked the idea and were eager to help. By the end of the week, we had a map, we had permits, we had a race! Accolades poured in the Monday after the race from participants, sponsors, and also from both the City of Oceanside and the City of Carlsbad. Each city wanted the marathon to be held within its own city limits next year.

Now the fun part started. How do we choose the right city? We decided on Carlsbad.

Seven

SCAMS AND SCOUNDRELS

The next couple of years after our move to Carlsbad proved to be beneficial to In Motion. We were steadily growing, adding new events regularly. The marathon, our number one event, was growing but not as quickly as I would've liked. I was doing all the sponsorship sales but wearing lots of other hats at the same time, so I was constantly looking for a good salesperson - someone who could focus entirely on selling sponsorship. I hired people whom I hoped would fit the bill, but none of them lasted very long, and none were very productive.

I had just about given up on ever finding a good salesperson when I was contacted by the president of a small sports marketing company in Orange County. He introduced himself—let's call him PM—as president of the Newport Beach marketing and advertising firm with the penchant for clients in sports-related businesses. He had heard good things about our marathon and had actually come down to Carlsbad to check it out and was impressed.

He supplied me with news clippings and photos of major events that he had produced, indicating that sports-related clients accounted for almost half of the company's billings last year.

Further articles indicated that his billings this year would reach $3.9 million. He invited my daughters and I to come up to Newport Beach and meet with him and his team.

Our first meeting was held on January 22, 1991, in their plush three-story office building. The walls were lined with pictures of PM with professional athletes, major sponsors, and promoters.

We would find out later that the office building where we met was actually borrowed from a relative who had the same last name but no other connection

Within a few days of our first meeting, I'd signed a contract with this new company to sell sponsorship and also produce a three-hour live telecast of our event. PM contacted me the first week, requesting my contracts with location TV station, KUSI and the Honda Dealership Association, so that he could take over working with these very important clients. Well... I had worked very hard to secure both these contracts, they both would require continuous oversight and management. At the time it made sense to me. So I turned them over.

PM had four salespersons working strictly on selling sponsorship for our marathon. They all got to work immediately and reported in weekly.

I had worked directly with the TV station in the past and had done all right, but I still had lots of other things to do. PM had assured me that he had years of experience in producing major television shows. My contract with Honda was solid. They had promised me new cars to the first-place male and female finishers. But there again, there was other work to be done.

The initial reports from PM and his crew were promising! Jack in the Box was interested in a $50,000 package and Lexus a $100,000 package until I reminded them that we already had Honda. Arrowhead was interested in sponsoring the wheelchair division, Health Net and Security Pacific wanted proposals and

Vons had offered to do end-aisle displays, gear bags, and all our printing.

By the end of March, I was getting a little nervous. A lot of money had been promised, but I still hadn't seen any hard dollars or signed contracts. Just to reassure myself, I had considered the possibility of taking out a second trust deed on my rental house. Real estate was increasing rapidly at that time, so I thought if I needed it, I could use that money to hold over until money started coming in from marathon sponsorships.

PM assured me that they would raise at least $360,000 in sponsorship, which would mean more than $200,000 in profit from the marathon. By the end of May, they had raised $340,000, according to PM, but we still had no signed contracts.

I was still nervous and seriously considered taking out seconds on my rental house and also on the condo in Cardiff I lived in with my new husband, Travis.

By August, I was really feeling uneasy and by October that uneasy feeling turned into total lack of trust in PM. I started to contact certain potential sponsors that I knew PM had been pitching. Several said they would work with me but not with PM, and some said they wouldn't be involved with the marathon if PM was involved. After hearing that, I needed to get back into selling sponsorship, but it was too late to be very effective.

It got worse. He had not only lied about his sales abilities, but he had also lied about his knowledge and experience in producing live telecasts. We were now thirty days out from the marathon, and he had done nothing. With my own limited experience and knowledge about live television, I jumped in and tried to pick up the pieces. I secured the camera locations on the course, recruited and signed the anchors for the show, and wrote most of the script.

On race day PM and his crew showed up late without the necessary antenna. They were scrambling, trying to find it. Fortunately, my son jumped in, took the antenna off his truck, and set it up for them. As a result of their weakness, the show was a half hour late starting, which cost us an additional $30,000 in ad time.

The $360,000 sponsorship money PM promised turned out to be less than $60,000. But the total loss turned out to be so much greater than that. At the end of the day I owed nearly $200,000. We were exhausted and devastated!

At 5:00 p.m. the day was finally over. I had five dollars in my pocket and knew I was almost out of gas. I stopped at a gas station, walked inside, and gave the clerk my last five dollars, then got in my car and drove home, forgetting to get any gas.

We spent the next couple of weeks licking our wounds and deciding what to do. We knew we would have to move out of our office. We couldn't pay our rent, and we couldn't pay our staff. Travis had a little corner in his office he could provide us, big enough for Christine and I to work in while Ellen did temp jobs in San Diego. We made a list of everyone we owed money to and tried to figure out how we were going to pay all our bills.

In the midst of all this dilemma, Ray Patchett, Carlsbad's city manager called to tell me that several people were in his office claiming to be the new owners of my marathon, the San Diego Marathon. They were names I didn't recognize, two from Los Angeles (attorneys), one from London, and one from Hong Kong. They were requesting the permits and plans from last year's marathon. Fortunately, Ray refused to turn anything over to them without my approval.

Hours later this same group contacted our host hotel, same story - they claimed to be the new owners of the San Diego Marathon. They wanted a copy of our sponsorship contract but were turned down by the hotel. They next called our timing company requesting contact information for all the San Diego Marathon participants, another denied request. They fought us for a while to gain control of the marathon until we filed suit and won a $1.06 million judgment against them. They soon lost interest and disappeared and I lacked the money to go after them.

PM denied any knowledge or relationship with any of these people, and we couldn't prove that he was involved, although we knew he was.

We were beginning to be contacted by creditors, so I decided to move ahead and borrow on my properties. The economy had taken a turn for the worse, and real estate values had dropped. Banks I had counted on six months earlier no longer wanted to talk to me. A friend of a friend introduced me to Oak Industries Funding in La Jolla, who then introduced me to a lender in the Golden Triangle who had two investors ready to move forward. The terms of the loans were outrageous; high interest rates and high points, but I felt it was my only option.

The other alternatives were to file bankruptcy or try and raise enough money to pay off the debt by seeking investors.

Filing bankruptcy was not an option so I immediately put together a prospectus to sell stock in my company. There appeared to be interest in the running community to invest in a historical community event. Unfortunately, within days of the release of my stock offering, the attempted hostile takeover of the San Diego Marathon hit the newspapers. The media was all over it. The result was a decision by most potential investors to back off.

I had already prepaid the ridiculous interest for the first six months of the loans. So guess what - I lost both properties. They had been taken by the lenders. I'd been taken again. I felt as though I was suddenly surrounded by scams and scoundrels.

Eight

How Did We Get through This?

In Motion was as broke as broke could be. But we weren't the only ones. The real estate boom of the early to mid-1980s was over. Property values were dropping, and unemployment was increasing. By 1990 and 1991, the country was in a recession, and unemployment continued to increase through June 1992.

We had to lay off everyone in our office, although Christine and Ellen and I still worked - we just didn't get paid.

We still had clients and contracts, but we had this unanticipated $200,000 debt that had to be paid, so any money that came in went right out. I had lost both our properties, so Travis and I started looking everywhere for something we could afford, but we kept getting turned down because of our terrible credit. We finally got lucky. We found a small apartment behind the Del Mar train station that was managed by a very nice couple whose daughter had worked with us on many events. She knew what had happened, and she put in a good word for us.

We promised each other we would stay there for only six months until we got back on our feet. Six months turned into five years, but we had learned to love our little place.

The pricey restaurants that lined the main streets in Del Mar were way out of our reach, but we found a little bar that worked for us. We shared a glass of wine and munched on the free homemade bread, that was our meal a couple nights a week for several years.

Travis had just signed a contract to manage a rundown building in Carlsbad. The owners wanted him to get it fixed up and then rent all the empty spaces. It was in really bad shape, so he hired Christine and I to do some of the work, like cleaning bathrooms and scrubbing toilets.

We did a good job, so he promoted us for our next task: paint the interior of one of the empty warehouses. That task was daunting. The warehouse was huge. We looked at the paintbrushes and decided there had to be a better way to get the job done.

Christine had an old pickup truck, so while she drove very, very slowly around the perimeter of the warehouse, I balanced myself carefully in the back of the truck with a roller in hand and lots of paint. Somehow, we got it done and we made a little money.

At this same time, we had thousands of T-shirts left over from races just stored away. We needed money to live on so we decided to try selling them at the Oceanside Swap Meet.

We loaded as many shirts as we could in my car and in Christine's truck and rushed to get a good spot at the swap meet. After a long day, Christine, Ellen, Pat, and I were tired but happy and had made enough to live on for a couple weeks.

So we packed up and headed for the parking lot but we couldn't find my car. We looked everywhere and finally went to the security stand and reported it stolen. The guard, with a strange look on his face, paused and said, "Did you happen to have a brown Ford sedan?"

I was relieved but then so embarrassed when he continued, "You left your car in the middle of the driveway this morning, blocking all of the sellers trying to get in to set up. Your engine was running, all four doors and your trunk wide open. Obviously, you were in a hurry to get set up."

He was not happy with me, but the good thing was I had left my keys in the ignition, so he could move my car.

Katie, Christine, Ellen, Lynn, Pat

• • •

Around this same time we were producing a multi-city event for Leo Burnett and their client, Keebler called Keebler Snack & Field.

Albertsons was a major sponsor of the event and provided anyone who attended with a twenty five dollar Albertsons gift card. At the end of the day, there was plenty of Keebler product as well as a number of Albertsons gift cards leftover.

After the event in Seattle, with Albertsons cards that had to be used in the Seattle area and with only a couple hours until our flight back to San Diego, we hit as many Albertsons stores as we could. We used the leftover gift cards to purchase toothpaste, shampoo, pasta, cereal, soup, tuna—anything that could be carried on our flight and stored in the overhead. That was before TSA.

We continued the struggle to increase our income and to chip away at the debt. I think I had called on just about every bank in San Diego. Christine and I would get dressed up, prepare a balance sheet and the profit & loss, and ask to see the bank manager. I really didn't even know what a balance sheet was, so I guessed at it. Invariably, the banker was either out for the day or smiled and said no thanks.

In Motion has had thousands of volunteers over the years; some stand out more than others, and one in particular can be remembered for saving our company. He was aware of our financial situation and was determined to help. He tried a number of things, but like us, he always hit a brick wall. Then one day he called and said he had set up a meeting for me with the vice president of North County Bank in Escondido.

The three of us had lunch the next day. The banker, soft spoken and a good listener started the conversation by asking me to talk about myself. He let me talk for a long time until I had answered all his questions. It was quiet for a few moments.

He looked at me and said, "I trust you. I am going to help you. There's some paperwork that you will have to supply, but nothing that will stand in the way. I will have a plan ready for you in a few days."

I struggled to keep from crying. After so many "no's", to hear not only a strong "yes" but even better, to hear "I trust you" meant the world to me! That meeting was twenty years ago, and I still get teary-eyed when I think of it today.

I provided the bank everything they requested, and they got me the plan. First they paid the $10,000 I owed the IRS for the foreclosure on my house. I always thought that was ridiculous that I could be charged taxes on a property that I lost, but that's how the IRS works.

Next they directed me to contact every debtor and negotiate with them to accept fifty cents on the dollar; many did. The bank then paid off in full the prize money so that all the winning athletes from that past year's Carlsbad Marathon were paid. Finally, they lent us the capital we needed to get up to speed, which we quickly did. We were able to pay off all our debt in three years and six months, including the loan from North County Bank. In Motion was debt free!

Starting line at the Union-Tribune Dr. Seuss Race for Literacy

Lynn Flangan

North County Bank is no longer in business, having been pur-chased by another bank. But as far as I'm concerned, Todd Twedt and North County Bank will always be heroes to me.

With their guidance and trust we were now able to really focus on our current clients which at that time included America's Finest City, Light the Night, and La Jolla Half Marathon, among others.

Nine

The Spirit of Joshua

It was late in the morning of the 2002 San Diego Marathon when most of the participants had finished running. We were starting to break down and clean up when I got a call on my radio from Todd Floyd, a long-time family friend and member of our extended event staff.

In a strained voice he said, "Lynn, where are you? I have someone you need to meet. He sounded upset, which concerned me, so I stopped what I was doing and went to meet him. Todd was waiting for me with a young girl whom I didn't recognize, and through his tears, he began to tell me her story.

Her name was Jill, and she had come to pick up her brother's medal and his shirt. I said, "Of course we can give those to you, but where is your brother?"

She softly explained to me that her brother, Josh Birnbaum, had registered and trained for the marathon but he wasn't there because he had been killed a few months before, on 9/11, at the World Trade Center.

Josh was a new employee at Cantor Fitzgerald, a well-known Wall Street company, and when he decided to run the San Diego

Marathon, his first, Jill promised that she would be there for him, to support him and to greet him at the finish line. She had made a commitment to her big brother whom she loved dearly. They were inseparable, and she meant to keep that commitment to him in spite of the tragedy that had changed that family forever.

She had climbed mountains to keep her commitment to her brother. Without telling her parents, she was able to scrape together enough money to buy a plane ticket. When she arrived in San Diego, she expected the marathon to be close by, not knowing that we had moved the marathon to Carlsbad, 30 miles from the airport. Jill had never heard of Carlsbad, but somehow she found her way north and arrived at the finish line very late, afraid she might have missed the whole thing. Determined not to let her brother down, she started searching for someone who could help her. Fortunately, Jill ran into Todd, who took control. She didn't tell her parents about her plans because she knew how upset they would be at the very thought of her getting on a plane when they were still reeling from the loss of their son.

"Joshua was my older brother, but he was more than that," said nineteen-year-old Jill. "He was my best friend in the world. When he signed up to do his first marathon, he asked me to come to San Diego to support him and to meet him at the finish line. I promised I would."

By now everyone on the staff had heard bits and pieces of Jill's story, and they were eager to meet her. They all stopped what they were doing and gathered around her. We held an impromptu but formal ceremony presenting Jill with her brother's medal, shirt, and bib number. She asked me to sign his bib number, which I did with a trembling hand and many tears.

A Life in Motion

When Jill first heard the news report on September 11, she called her mother right away because Jill knew that Josh's father, Sam, worked in the World Trade Center complex just across the street from Josh in the World Trade Center. I remember saying, "Tell me Daddy's okay." Her mom said, "Daddy's okay, but Josh is missing."

Josh had seconds to call his mother to say goodbye to her and to ask her to say goodbye to Sam and to Jill and tell them all how much he loved them. Sam watched from his office window as the second plane struck the second tower and into the floor where he knew his son worked.

Josh had run with the wrong crowd in high school and was into the club scene but when he was nineteen, everything changed. It was like a light switch went on in his head. He started going to Narcotics Anonymous and kicked his drug habit, then enrolled in a community college in New York. The next step was being accepted at Columbia. No one thought he could get into an Ivy League school, but Josh was determined. He graduated with a degree in economics.

On May 18, 2001, three days after graduation, Josh became one of the two applicants selected from the thousand who had applied for a job at Cantor Fitzgerald as an assistant bond trader.

"God gave Josh five years to show what he could make of life and of himself," said Jill. "He could've died many times before he went straight, but he made it."

After the race and that day was over, I could not put Jill or Joshua or their mother out of my mind. I'm a mother. I have a son who had similar problems, who could've been Joshua. Like Josh, my son, after some very rough teenage years, had turned his life around. During those early hours of 9/11, my son was in a plane flying from San Francisco to Pennsylvania. I couldn't reach him that terrible day, didn't know where he was or what flight he was on, but after hours of agony, we got his call. His plane had landed safely. He was safe.

I just couldn't get that out of my mind. I knew the heartaches that a mother goes through when her children are hurting or lost. I could just imagine how she must be suffering, so I had to reach out to her.

I found her phone number on Joshua's marathon entry form, and I called her. We had a wonderful conversation, and from that day forward, Marcel and I have been good friends She is a kind, loving, and resilient woman, a friend you can laugh and cry with. We may go for months without talking, but when we do, it's like we've always been together.

Travis and I have stayed with Marcel and Sam in New York. We attended Jill's wedding, and we have met a number of their friends who also lost a child to 9/11. They were all employees of Cantor Fitzgerald. Several of their friends asked us to help them find a way to keep their children alive just as they felt we had done for Joshua.

On one visit to New York, Travis and I stayed with the Birnbaums and slept in Joshua's room. His books, his music, and other memorabilia spoke to us of Joshua. Our tears came quickly when we saw his marathon medal and the San Diego Marathon bib number he would have worn on race day.

We were so impressed by Jill that after that first year we estab-lished an annual Spirit of Joshua Award, an award that was presented by the Birnbaums every year for ten years. This award went to someone who had overcome incredible odds to get to the starting line and to the finish line of our marathon. These award winners were amazing people who also established a bond and a friendship with the Birnbaums.

A Life in Motion

Jill and her husband, Richie, have two beautiful little girls. We have a special bond with the Birnbaums and the Spirit of Joshua Award winners. I feel very fortunate to have been able to play a small role in their lives.

I also feel fortunate to have a staff who are always ready to lend a hand, with kindness and compassion no matter how tired they are or how much work lies ahead of them. They are good people.

I was recently in touch with the Birnbaums, and I asked Jill about those who had been awarded the Spirit of Joshua Award. She emailed me her thoughts. She talked about Van Ballew, the first winner, a man of great strength and courage in the final stages of ALS, who crossed the finish line in a wheelchair.

She talked about Deanna Brix, a young woman who planned to do the marathon in her wheelchair accompanied by her service dog, Malachi. The Birnbaums were planning to track her progress online, but in the later part of the race, Deanna could not be found. Jill went out on the course with one of the Harley drivers, and they found Deanna stranded, her dog's feet bleeding badly from the run. So Jill and several other volunteers decided to push Deanna the rest of the way and cross the finish line with Deana, her dog on her lap. Jill decided at that moment that next year she would complete her first half marathon and really honor her brother and his spirit.

Jill ended her thoughts with these words: "All of the winners have had a life-altering impact on me but none as much as your family, Lynn. You made all the beauty and memorialization possible. And for that, I am forever grateful. Thank you for taking Todd's call over the radio that January in 2002, and for allowing us to be a part of your family."

She signed, "All my love and gratitude, Jill."

Ten

DAD

It was about this time that my Dad died and my brothers, my sister and I were suffering. I wrote the following message to my children. I was crying when I wrote it, so I folded the tear-soaked letter and stuck it in a drawer and didn't take it out for years.

No matter how ready we all thought we were, when his death came, it rolled across us with great crushing pain, a grayness, sharp and slashing as any pain I had ever felt.

We cling fast to each other, afraid to let go and face the pain alone. We stayed too long, and we repeated the same stories. Then finally we turned from each other and went timidly back into the outside world, to face our individual sorrow and to shed our own tears.

Much of what I am today is because of my father. He could never say, "I love you," although I never doubted that he did. On two or three occasions during the past few years, I have stepped way out of my usual comfort zone with him and said, "Dad, I love you," and he mumbled, "I love you too."

I try very hard to be more open and verbal with you, my children, but it's not easy, and I regret that I haven't said these words more often. If I could, I would tell you every day that you are each my life, that I have loved you from the first moment I saw you, and my love for each of you has grown stronger every day since those first moments. My love is fierce and protective and nonjudgmental, and it knows no boundaries. Like my father, my words often fail me, but I hope that my actions fill you with the knowledge of my love.

In the last year, my father's health deteriorated, and he became weaker each day, but he still was eager to see each of us and would listen for a car in the driveway of their mobile home. He would always be at the kitchen door when I came in, even though the walk from the living room may have been a struggle. After a half hour of idle conversation about everything from politics to OJ, he would say, "You'll stay for dinner, won't you?" I would say, "No, Dad, I have to get home. Travis will be home soon," and then we would go back to our conversation. A few minutes later, he would struggle out of his chair and head back to the kitchen, where he would call to me, "I'm fixing pork chops for dinner; you'll stay, won't you?" And of course I would stay because he was telling me he loved me, and I needed to hear that.

Why share this today when the urge has been there for so long? Maybe because my father died this weekend and I am struggling to sort through my feelings and to maintain my normal routine without picking up the phone every hour to say to you, "Please come hold my hand,

and better yet, rock me in your arms like a child and tell me everything will be all right. But you are the children, and I am the parent, so I put the phone back and refrain from calling you because you have your own lives and are dealing with your own grief, and I will not intrude. It's not because you wouldn't come, I know each of you would, and you would stay with me until the wave of sorrow passes, but it's my own stubborn nature, my need to be strong and independent that stops me. I wish I could be different, but I probably never will be, so I am here, alone, mourning my father, his passing, and the warm protection of an innocent childhood.

We all knew the end was near and John, Mark, Chris, and Mary Denise and I dealt with it in our usual way, with lighthearted humor and goodwill, firmly convinced that we were prepared and would handle his departure in a mature and rational manner because you know us so well and you share the Coseo humor.

I know you won't be shocked to hear that at one of our pre-need funeral planning meetings, we all collapsed in uncontrolled laughter when one of us suggested tying dad to the top of Uncle Raymond's car and returning his body to Michigan for burial. At another such meeting, we voted to see who had the courage to broach the subject of cremation with Dad, knowing his traditional Catholic viewpoint. John, being the eldest, was elected, and we gave him lots of advice on how to go about it such as "Dad, would you like cremation, I mean Cremora, in your coffee." And, oh, by the way, not surprisingly, John never found the courage to bring it up, and Mary Denise, Dad's Harrisville baby, was the one to settle the issue.

Upon my Dad's passing, my three brothers took his ashes to Mount Mariah, a beautiful, isolated spot in the forest looking down on Hubbard Lake, where we had grown up. A few years later, my sister and I and our daughters had the responsibility of taking Mom's ashes to Hubbard Lake to join the man she loved.

Mt. Marriah with Dad's and Mom's Ashes

Alice, My kind gentle mother, is missed everyday, and is loved by anyone who had the good fortune of knowing her.

Eleven

WHAT ELSE DO WE DO

When people hear the name, In Motion, they think of "the running people," and they are correct. Our primary business is running. We have done hundreds and hundreds of running events over the years, but we are much more than that. Here are just a few of the out-of-the-norm events we have done:

- The first Dinner Dance under the stars on the new top deck of the San Diego Convention Center.
- A Bed Race for Sharp Hospital. Not only did we put on the event on, but we also entered a team of our four fastest employees pushing a gurney with Ellen being the patient on the gurney.
- A one-mile walk in the Gaslamp called "Walk a Mile in Her Shoes." It was a fundraiser for a YWCA women's shelter. The walk was just for men wearing very high heels. The first challenge for us was finding shoes that were big enough for the men's big feet and then jamming their feet into these shoes. Second challenge? Keeping the men upright as they hobbled through the streets. The event was held on a Friday night

during Happy Hour so there were lots of hooters and hollerers to keep the men moving.

- San Diego's only Hot Air Balloon Festival, which celebrated the opening of Rancho Penisquitos, a new housing development in San Diego. We were not responsible for inflating or flying the hot air balloons, but we were involved in just about every other aspect of the event.
- Convention runs. We did, and still do, produce private runs for conventions, big and small. Our first convention run was for the top five hundred advertisers in the United States and was held on the beach at the Hotel Del Coronado. The attendees were a very competitive group, so everything had to be perfect, and it was. The only thing we couldn't control was the heated disagreements among the convention attendees over who beat whom.
- America's Cup. Although none of us knew much about sailing, we were very involved in America's Cup when it came to San Diego from the opening night party at Horton Plaza to the closing night Poor Man's Ball and the in-between events, a bike ride and the America's Cup Walk across the Coronado Bridge.

One of our more challenging events was when we designed and produced an event for Road Runner Sports called the Overland 122 Relay. It was a brutal 122-mile relay from the desert to the top of Palomar Mountain and on to the ocean. Teams of five or ten runners took on the challenge, which started in Borrego Springs on Friday afternoon and hopefully finished on Sunday afternoon in Oceanside.

Our staff went to Borrego Springs Thursday afternoon to get everything ready for the Friday start. We were staying in a nice hotel with air conditioning, and planned to meet for dinner at six o'clock. Several of us came out of our rooms at the same time and found ourselves face-to-face with a large rattlesnake slithering down the hall. We were not sure if he was planning to have dinner with us or just looking for a cool spot to hang out. Dinner was delayed until hotel security came and removed the snake.

It was nonstop for the next forty-eight hours for the teams, the staff, and the volunteers. Some of the lucky ones got to take a short nap now and then, but most of us did not even get that.

The slower teams started the race first, usually between one and two o'clock on Friday afternoon with the temperature well over a hundred degrees. The really fast teams started hours later, after dark, and they usually caught up with the slower teams by morning.

Each team was given a list of required gear, which included things such as a fully equipped first aid kit, energy replacement drinks, at least four gallons of water per runner, headlamps, trash bags, proof of insurance, ice, and reflective vests. All vans had to be checked out by a staff member to make sure they had every item on the list before their team could start the race.

The first half of the race covered a remote area with little com- munication available. Cell phones didn't work out there. Our staff had rented a few satellite phones in case of an emergency. The teams were well informed and consistently reminded that if team members went down, their teammates were responsible for getting them to the nearest medical facility, which could be seventy to eighty miles away. That happened several times during the event, and the downed runner was transported and treated for dehydration and heat exhaustion. None of them wanted to quit, and after being treated, each insisted on rejoining his or her team.

After that first year, word got out about how difficult the event was, how dangerous it was, and how much fun it was. The next year the event name was changed to Wild Miles, the course differed some, but most teams returned and more prepared than before. Some of them came with their own EMT equipped to start IVs whenever needed on their downed teammate. When a less experienced team needed help for a downed runner, and they had no EMT, negotiations began between teams. I'm not sure what the deals were, and we didn't ask as long as everyone was okay.

We did the event for a few years and never lost anyone, but we came close. My husband, Travis, his good friend and fellow Jeep aficionado, Pete, along with several of their buddies would drive their Jeeps each year up and down the hills all night to locate any lost runners.

The teams absolutely loved Wild Miles. We still get calls from teams who want to know when we are going to do it again or how they can get in. Unfortunately, we had to make a tough decision. The liability risk was just too great to continue the fun.

Another one of our favorite events was one I mentioned earlier, Keebler Snack and Field. Leo Burnett, a Chicago-based ad agency, contracted with us to produce a free children's fitness event for one of their clients, Keebler. They wanted an event that would feature Keebler's Ernie the Elf as a really good guy with a great product. The event was held in five major cities along the West Coast. The concept was to have a kids sports day with well-known athletes offering clinics. The sports were basketball, baseball, football, track & field, and soccer. The athletes included people like Bill Walton for basketball, Juli Veee for soccer, Billy Mills for running, and Carney Lansford for baseball. The events were free to kids and parents, and in addition to meeting and working with big-name athletes, the kids got their fill of yummy Keebler cookies.

Kids and parents loved the events, and so did our staff. We traveled together to each event. The Leo Burnett people entertained us at nice restaurants for dinner every night - In Motion, Keebler and the athletes. We had great conversations, and I even got to wear Carney Lansford's World Series ring for a few minutes.

My Leo Burnett contact, Linda Morgenstern, invited me to spend a couple of days in Chicago meeting their people and learning how their agency operated. It was a wonderful opportunity, and I learned a lot. Snack and Field was a one-year contract between Leo Burnett and Keebler, so after the last city, we all parted with fond memories and newfound friends. Keebler chose to remain with us and sponsored our kids race at the Carlsbad Marathon, Keebler Kids Marathon Mile, for many years.

During that time, we worked with the supermarkets who carried Keebler products. I learned all about the costs and importance of end caps and got pretty good at doing store checks.

Ernie the Keebler Elf often appeared, along with the Keebler cookie truck, at our events. Because Ellen was the shortest person in our office, she often had to appear in the Ernie costume at events and at schools. The little kids loved her. I think they thought she was real, and they couldn't resist tackling her. It was pretty funny seeing her lying on her back with her legs up in the air yelling for help. We always made sure we had someone close by to get her upright again.

Probably one of our most unusual events was a small walk we did for the Child Abuse Prevention Foundation and that involved inmates at the Richard J. Donovan Correctional Facility in San Diego County. The Child Abuse Prevention Foundation had a relationship with Donovan and when the prison warden learned of the walk, knew the inmates, many whom have children of their own, would want to help. Obviously, they couldn't participate in the walk because they were incarcerated, but they still wanted to help.

We were asked by a prison men's group to assist them in raising money for the event. The warden asked us to come to the prison to meet with this group and give them some ideas. We had no idea what to expect but wanted to give these men a chance to participate in a positive community event. The meeting was set, we were told how to get there, and we were told what not to wear - blue, red, or jeans.

Donovan is in a remote part of San Diego County, near the Mexico border, about fifty miles from our office. The closer we got to the prison, the more nervous we got. We were stopped at the main gate, where my car was searched, then we were escorted into the main building, where we were each required to sign a release stating that if we were held hostage, the prison would not negotiate for our release.

Ellen, Christine, and I along with the other women in our group signed the release. We had a little time before our meeting with the men's group, so the warden asked if we would like to tour the facility. Of course we accepted the invitation. We were handed a safety vest, explaining that these had to be worn in the maximum security area because sometimes inmates spit at anyone within their range.

We entered the maximum security area which had between fifteen and twenty small cells on all four sides of the room. We were suddenly surrounded by the worst of the worst, each in his own cell. The noise was deafening. Not only did they spit; some also screamed obscenities. The guards were safe inside a glass structure in the center of the room. We knew we were safe but couldn't wait to get out of there. In spite of our fear, we couldn't help but feel sorry for these men. How could keeping them in this terrible environment prepare them for ever returning to a normal life?

After touring some of the workshops, cafeteria, and the library, it was time to meet with the men's group. We found this group to be cordial and eager to be involved. It was clear they wanted to do something to benefit the children at Child Protective Services.

Together we came up with a plan that would work for them. They would ask their families and friends and even some of the guards to pledge money for the number of push-ups they did, or sit-ups, or planks, or the number of laps they ran.

Next we walked through the yard, where hundreds of inmates were lifting weights, doing push-ups, running laps, and chatting with each other. They seem to be happy to see us and were polite

The prison had a print shop, and they offered to print the thirty thousand entry forms needed for the walk. Christine made regular trips to Donovan for the next few months to meet with the head of the prison print shop to approve the items they were printing for us. Fortunately, she didn't have to go into maximum security again.

The event benefited the Child Abuse Prevention Foundation, but I'm quite certain that the inmates benefited too.

The experience strengthened my belief that our judicial system needed to change.

Twelve

FAMILY AND FITNESS

I'm quite sure that I'm one of the luckiest people in the world. That doesn't mean that my family and I have lived a charmed life. Far from it. We certainly have had our share of accidents, divorces, financial problems, illnesses, and losses. But we always come together as one to support and console each other and to help each other out whenever needed.

We cry together, we laugh together, we pray together, and we certainly party together. We celebrate every holiday, birthday, graduation, anniversary, host going away parties and coming home parties, and we have worked so well together all these years.

Occasionally people inquire if we ever fight. Ask someone like Kathleen, Ellen's childhood friend who has been a part of our extended event staff for over 30 years. She and others may tell you about the time long ago when Ellen and Christine had an argument after leaving an event. Nobody recalls what the argument was about, but it is rumored that Ellen made Christine walk home! We laugh at the idea of this exchange because not only are we not fighters, we're also not yellers! In fact, we're often complimented on our calm demeanor and collaborative nature even in the face of challenges.

How do we stay so close? How do we work so well together? I think the answer is that each generation was taught certain values: love, kindness, compassion, and integrity. My parents passed these values on to my brothers and sister and me, and we have passed them on to our children. Our children are now passing them on to their children. We have also instilled a strong work ethic in the younger generations. If you've been to any of our events, you have seen or experienced these virtues and the work ethic of our grandchildren. Just look around, and you'll see what I mean.

Caleb, my grandson and my daughter Katie's oldest was blessed with a beautiful voice. He's been known to begin a race with his amazing rendition of the national anthem, in a voice that brings the crowd to tears. After which he comes down off the announcer's tower to help out wherever he's needed. He's currently teaching middle school in an impoverished area of Louisiana for Teach for America.

Katie's daughter, Saralyn, is a born leader and at any given event can be found overseeing a specific area with lots of volunteers. She's currently finishing up her undergrad at Vanguard University of Southern California with a degree in Psychology. She's looking forward to pursuing further studies in horse therapy.

Ellen's son and our first grandchild, Jordan, is very much like his mother, gentle with a friendly disposition and one who considers no task too hard. Jordan earned his degree at Cal State Long Beach and is finishing up the classes needed for an advanced degree in physical therapy. Having a physical therapist in a family of runners is very convenient.

Hannah, Christine's daughter, first began coming to the office when she was just five days old, When she was eight, she was eight, she decided she was ready to drive one of the golf carts. She took down a few booths in the expo tent, but nobody was hurt! Everyone loved her and thought it was pretty funny, so she got away with it that time. She later designed a new system for collecting and returning runners' gear that we use to this day. Hannah recently finished her master's degree in Conservation Leadership at Colorado State University and is currently in Panama with the Peace Corps where she'll be for the next two years,

Myles, Christine's son, is a freshman at Cal Poly San Luis Obispo. Until he left for college in the summer of 2017 he was a staple at every In Motion event. Always eager to help with a funny and loving disposition, his departure to college was a loss to the team. Myles and I always have always shared a love of reading. When he read his first Harry Potter book, he asked his mother for a second copy so that he could come to the office after school every day so the two of us could read it together.

Pat's children, Luca and Michaela, not only work at most In Motion event they also help at their dad's Butterfly Farm and Luca and Michaela Nursery. They are both knowledgeable and can teach anyone all about the life cycle of butterflies.

Travis' oldest child, Jenifer's daughter, Kadie was always a familiar face in the merchandise booth at the marathon. That was until she graduated from Berkeley in 2016 with a double major in chemical engineering and computer animation. After internships in Singapore, Chicago, and at Disney, she was accepted her dream job at Disney, and is now working on a movie that premieres in 2018.

All my children have a role at In Motion, and though my two youngest, Ellen and Christine, oversee the day-to-day, Katie and Pat have been and continue to be an important part of our success.

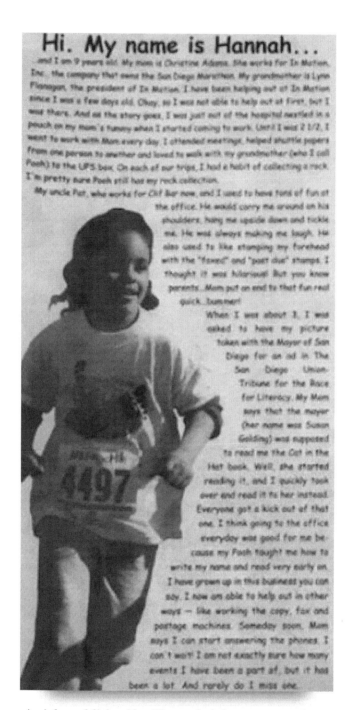

Article published by Hannah Adams at age nine

At any event you're likely to see my grandchildren.
Here they are:
Micaela, Saralyn, Jordan, Hannah, Myles, Caleb and Luca.

My son, Pat, often takes a day off from running his Butterfly Farm to make sure pace cars are where they need to be. He also often drives the press truck which can be very challenging making sure the photographers get good shots while not running over any runners. He is fast on a forklift and his institutional knowledge of events is amazing.

Among many other things, come event weekend, Ellen makes sure all our volunteers are trained and in place at the starting line, the finish line, and all along the course. She has no trouble recruiting volunteers because she treats everyone with such respect. They love her.

Christine will be on the phone with PD to ensure that the course is closed to all traffic and we're good to start the race. She gets the call and signals the announcer: "We are good to go." First come the Harleys, then the pace cars, then the press truck, then the wheelchairs, then the walkers and runners!

Katie, well she could be anywhere, from announcing, to staffing a key support station, or to her newest role, riding on a Harley and overseeing the entire race course.

What I love about all my kids is that they know it all, and can step into any role and perform its tasks, perfectly.

Our family's commitment to running may set us apart. I didn't always think of myself as being an athlete or even being fit. When I was young, I played softball with my brothers and the neighborhood boys. We swam in Hubbard Lake in the summer and skated on the frozen pond in the winter. When my children were in elementary school, I learned to play tennis, and I got pretty good at it. That's when I realized how competitive I was. Being okay wasn't good enough. I played hard. I played to win.

But then I discovered running, and there was no turning back. I went from running two-to-three miles three or four times a week to running forty-to-fifty miles a week in a relatively short period of time. My kids were way ahead of me. Katie, now in high school played field hockey, volleyball, and ran track and field. Pat played hockey (on concrete), baseball, and soccer and in his adult life when on to create the Clif Bar Cyclocross team. Ellen and Christine both excelled in running and were winning every race they entered.

Soon we were a family of runners with trophies piling up all over our house. Ellen was getting ready for high school and was being recruited by coaches from several local schools. But she and Christine preferred to stay at Mission Bay High School, where they both excelled in cross country and track.

My first husband was no longer part of the team, we were separated, but my children and I had stayed together for many, many miles - wonderful miles with wonderful memories. Our first marathon together was Marine Corps in Washington, DC. Katie, Pat, Ellen, and I had trained together for months for this big day. Oprah Winfrey was also running the Marine Corps Marathon that year. Because of all the extra security and the extra media she attracted everyone had to line up and wait at the starting line in the rain and freezing temperatures for forty five minutes while Oprah finished her interviews. We all made it to the finish line, but I needed help getting through the mud in the recovery area. Fortunately, two nice marines, one on each side, pulled me out of the mud and carried me to a dry area. It was a learning experience. We decided we would never let that happen at one of our events.

Our running family extends far beyond my four children and me.

In 1986 I was conducting one of my first committee meetings for the Heart of San Diego Marathon when a good-looking guy in a three-piece suit walked in the room, and my heart skipped a beat. I wasn't sure who he was, but I learned later he was a volunteer at the Heart Association, his name was Travis Burleson, he was from Houston, Texas, and he was a real estate broker and served on a special committee to oversee In Motion's performance with the marathon.

The CEO of the Heart Association had asked him to attend the meetings and report back to him. After the meeting, most of the committee went across the street for a drink at a neighborhood bar. It was a cordial gathering, with a number of younger people on the committee, mostly women who all had an eye on Travis.

Travis and I both stayed for a while after the meeting, just talking and a little getting-to-know-you. He mentioned that he was single and that he had no interest in dating. His focus was on his children and on his career in commercial real estate.

I said, "Great. I'm not interested in dating either." He was a runner and at the next meeting we agreed to meet at Fletcher Cove later that week to go for a run after work. We ended up going for the run and then to dinner and talking for hours.

Travis's reports back to the CEO must have been good. We were spending more and more time together, and not just talking about the marathon. Two years later we were married. That was twenty-nine years ago. We are still very much together and very much in love.

But our family extends beyond that. Travis and I have seven children between us, as well as thirteen grandchildren and two great-grandchildren, and all of them have participated in one or more of our races, as have my brothers and lots of nieces and nephews. Even my sister walked our half marathon, in spite of a severe debilitating illness, Ankylosing Spondylitis. I had the joy of training with her to help her reach her goal. I am so proud of her.

Two of my elderly aunts flew out from Detroit one year to see the marathon. Aunt Ethel and Aunt Helen were able to walk the

5K we had in conjunction with the marathon that year. They had never done anything like this and were so proud to go back to Detroit with a race T-shirt and a medal.

It hasn't been all fun and games. My stepdaughter, Jenifer, was diagnosed in 2007 with leiomyosarcoma, a rare cancer with a 5 percent chance of survival beyond five years. We were all devas-tated, but she is a fighter. Her first surgery required the removal of one kidney and a section of her vena cava. Five years later, her cancer was back attacking her hip and her liver, but she was still fighting and survived another round of surgery and radiation.

Jenifer had been an athlete and had done several triathlons and then, between surgeries, she decided to participate in our half marathon in 2012.

Granddaughter Kadie with her mother, Jenifer

Our Carlsbad Marathon sponsors' reception is held a few nights before the marathon. It's a wonderful evening held in an upscale hotel with dinner, drinks, music and a few hundred guests. This is where we acknowledge all the sponsors of the event and we also introduce the Heroes of the Marathon, those very special people who have overcome major obstacles to be able to participate in the marathon or the half.

Unbeknownst to Jenifer, she had been selected as one of our Heroes of the Marathon. She was speechless when the MC called her to the stage to receive her award. She reached her goal five years ago when she and her sister, Leslee, crossed the half mara-thon finish line to the roar of the crowd and with the pride of her family.

Her cancer is back again, this time in her lungs, but she is not giving up. She is strong, determined, beautiful, and still teaching at Valley Middle School. And she is even running a little.

Running runs deep in our souls. Not only has it been a favorite pastime for our family, but it's been one of our ways of giving back to our community. The hundreds of events we have done have raised many millions of dollars for various charities, and we have introduced hundreds of thousands of people to a healthy lifestyle. What more could we ask for?

Thirteen

THE DEFINITION OF SUCCESS

I learned very early on that there was more to being successful than just making money. Of course making money with each of our events is important. We have mortgages, we have employees, we have to pay taxes, insurance, and utilities, just like every other business.

But our real success is not measured by the money we make. It is measured by the good things we are able to do - big things and small.

For example, our events help so many nonprofit organizations do amazing work to help hundreds of thousands of people in our community and across the country. We have had the unique honor of working with hundreds of nonprofit organizations for nearly thirty-five years. We have worked hand in hand to help them raise the money they need to meet their goals.

Some of these organizations are huge, and the money they make each year with our events helps fight diseases like breast cancer, leukemia, Alzheimer's, and diabetes. It's always a good feeling at the end of the day to know that we played a role in helping that organization reach its goals.

Besides working with these popular, well-known organizations, we have had the opportunity to help create dozens of new organizations. Often a group of friends or maybe a parent want to do an event to raise money and awareness for a child or spouse or a friend suffering from a serious, little-known disease.

I met Shari and her seven-year-old son, Parker, twelve years ago. He had been battling a rare and life-threatening autoimmune disease, juvenile dermatomyositis (JM). Her goal was to run our marathon and raise $50,000 in pledges for Cure JM, a national non-profit organization. Her commitment was contagious. There was no question she would reach her goal and we would do whatever we could to help her. Parker is now a handsome young man. So far, his disease has not stopped him. And it hasn't stopped Shari either. She continues to fight this disease by setting up running programs throughout the country. Members in each program raise money by participating in their local marathon and getting pledges to help support Cure JM.

Here's another example. Aurora was a major challenge for us when she showed up to register for our In Motion Fit training program. We quickly realized that she was legally blind. She ran with a cane and a guide who ran right in front of her. She had never run in a race, but she was convinced she could do it. She couldn't drive, of course, but she assured us that the 4:00 a.m. bus stop was near her house, and with a couple of transfers, she could get to our 7:00 a.m. training session every Saturday.

She was vice president of the Blind Community Center of San Diego and wanted to raise money and awareness for that organization.

We helped with arranging transportation for her and encouraged our members to keep an eye on her, which many of them did. She never missed a training session and was there before dawn on marathon morning. It was a very long race day, but she made it to the finish line and has stayed with us for many years. When I feel her soft hands on my face and hear her voice calling, "Miss Lynn, is that you?" I know it's Aurora.

In a letter she sent me several years ago, she said, "Through the marathon I have gained self-esteem, maintained my physical fitness, participated in many other sports, and I motivated others to be more involved. Most of all, I am not afraid to accept a challenge."

There have been so many times in my career when people have crossed my path like this - people passionate about their cause, people you just can't say no to. You have to get involved. You have to help.

Liz is one of those people, one I will never forget. She came by my office one day unannounced and asked to speak to me. She introduced herself and began to talk about her son, Christopher. He was a middle school student, thirteen years old. A year ago, while running during PE, he had collapsed and gone into total cardiac arrest. In other words, he died. By the grace of God, his coach started CPR immediately and the EMTs got him to the hospital in time to save his life, at least temporarily. The doctors told Liz and her husband that their son had a very serious heart condition and his chance of survival was slim.

Several months later a young boy Christopher's age was in a terrible, fatal accident. Thanks to this boy's amazing parents, Christopher is alive and is now the recipient of this other boy's heart. Liz wanted to tell this story, to honor the donor and his family, to spread the word about the importance of organ transplants, and to honor everyone who had played a role in Christopher's survival.

I hid my tears and then called everyone else into my office to meet Liz and hear her story. "Let's put together a relay. It's a lot of work to fit the relay into the Carlsbad Marathon, but we can do it." Everyone agreed. Liz gave us the list of who she wanted on that team: the coach, the EMTs, the nurses and the doctors who treated him in the emergency room, the doctors and nurses who did the transplant, and finally the parents of the boy who donated the heart.

The plan was that the course would be divided up among the team members. After completing their individual sections, everyone would meet at mile 25.5. Christopher, now strong enough to complete a mile, joined his lifesavers at this point, and hand in hand they marched the last mile and crossed the finish line together. Christopher is now a Stanford graduate, doing well, and Liz continues the battle for organ transplants.

We don't always produce huge public events. We do lots of middle-sized events, and occasionally we throw things together on the spur of the moment for someone who needs us but certainly can't afford the normal costs like for Paul, a member of our In Motion Fit training program. His twenty-year-old daughter had stage IV cancer, and her insurance didn't cover the special treatment she needed. Everyone in the office got involved. With Paul's help we were able to secure a permit to put on a run at Liberty Station in just two weeks, a permit that ordinarily would take months to secure. We begged our vendors to donate their services and got the word out to the thousands of runners and walkers in our database. We got T-shirts donated and lots of pos-trace goodies to feed all the participants.

All the entry fees went to the cause. Thousands of dollars were raised - enough to pay for Paul's daughter to have her next procedure done and to prolong her life for almost a year.

Then there was D. J., a well-known local athlete who usually placed in the top ten at any local race. He sometimes served as an announcer at running events in Southern California and Arizona.

Late one night, exhausted, on his way home from a long race weekend in Phoenix, DJ fell asleep at the wheel, lost control of his car, rolled over, and tumbled to the bottom of a canyon that couldn't be seen from the highway. Hours later a truck driver spotted DJ's car lights and called the Highway Patrol. DJ was unconscious and badly injured.

We got word the next day and immediately started making plans. He had spent several weeks in the hospital and was facing months of rehab. He was weak, had difficulty walking, and had very little insurance, but he was alive. As soon as he was back in town, we asked him to meet us at Mission Bay for a barbecue.

He arrived, expecting to see the In Motion people and a couple other good friends and instead found hundreds of runners bringing food, good wishes, and money to help with his medical bills. There was lots of joy that night.

But many times, it's just little things we get to do. Giving shoes to a new member of In Motion Fit when she tearfully admitted that she couldn't afford to buy running shoes. Her sixteen-year-old daughter had run away, gotten into trouble with the wrong gang, and ended up in jail. This anguished mother was working hard, and every penny she made went to save her daughter - to get her child out of jail and back on the right track and to pay for a good attorney.

She cried when we quietly presented her with a brand new pair of running shoes. "Your training program is the only good thing in my life right now," she mumbled quietly.

Collecting blankets for the homeless and then encouraging some of the homeless to participate in one of our events did make a difference. Managing a water station was so inspiring that some of them actually stopped smoking and started running. I consider that success for us and for them.

I believe one of our biggest successes is our training program, In Motion Fit. We started the program in 1995 and since then have helped thousands complete a life goal - running or walking a full or half marathon. I marvel at the numbers of people who have stayed with us and come back year after year. They share what Fit has done for them, how it has changed their lives, and how they are healthier, happier people because of it.

At the 2017 America's Finest City Half Marathon, a woman approached me and asked if I was Lynn Flanagan. I didn't recognize her, but she seemed to recognize me and said she had always wanted to meet me. She referred to me as the Mother of Running in San Diego and thanked me for saving her marriage.

I learned that ten years earlier her marriage was on the rocks. Before she and her husband moved ahead with their planned divorce, they agreed to try one more thing - train and run a marathon together. They joined In Motion Fit and trained together religiously for twenty-six weeks, then conquered the marathon together. The intensity, camaraderie, and the knowledge that they could do anything brought them closer than they had ever been. Their marriage not only survived, but it's healthy and grows stronger every day.

It's not unusual for someone I don't recognize to approach me and introduce themselves as someone who has been or still is a member of In Motion Fit. They just want to say thanks for what Fit has done for them.

I was waiting for my appointment with my physical therapist recently when a familiar face came out of an appointment with the same therapist. Bill was a longtime member of Fit. He had been with us from the beginning and stayed on as an assistant coach for many years. I hadn't seen him in many years. We chatted for a few minutes then he left for another appointment and I went back to my magazine. Moments later he returned to say "I want you to know that my time with Fit were the best years of my life." He hugged me and left.

I look back on the years I struggled to keep the company going. The sleepless nights: Did I do the right thing? Should I have accepted an offer to buy the company? Should I have given up and pursued a "real job?"

But now I have the answer. I am successful! I created a successful company, a company that does good things for people, a company that is well respected in the community.

I'm proud of the work we've done, but I'm even prouder of the amazing children I raised. They are kind, caring, generous adults who work hard carrying on traditions we established.

A recent letter came from Laura Farmer Sherman, executive director of Susan G. Komen San Diego, written on her last day at Komen before her retirement.

> I tried to say goodbye and thanks to you all for the more
> than a decade of our partnership. I just couldn't do it. I got
> close to where you are all standing but the big crybaby in me
> stopped me. I want you to know that I will always love,
> admire, and respect all of you. For your ethics, your can-do
> attitude, your hard work, your attitudes, and your just all
> around badass aura, and Lynn, that all started with you.
>   And I thank you from the bottom of my heart.
>   Love to you all,
>   Laura

If there was any doubt that we had succeeded, Laura confirmed it that day.

Fourteen

Remember That Time?

After having been in business for more than thirty-six years and having done hundreds of events, we have plenty of interesting stories: people we've met along the road, boo-boos that have happened, mistakes we've made.

When we're all together, invariably one of us says, "Remember that time…"

Here are a few of our favorites.

Remember the time the press truck, loaded with reporters, ran out of gas in the middle of the race? By the time we were able to refuel, the race was over, and the reporters had missed the finish.

Trains and trolleys are always a potential problem. There was a year Olympian Steve Scott, was running in one of our major races that crossed the train tracks. We were certain we had reviewed the schedules and knew there would be no problems. I was in the pace car followed very closely by Steve Scott and ten other elite athletes from around the world. As we approached the rails, the light and the whistles suddenly went on. The unexpected train was fast approaching. As the pace car, I had crossed the rail, but I could see that the lead pack would not make it. They will be held up for at least a minute or two, which would totally throw them off. My mind was racing.

"My career is over, I'll never put on another race, I should go home right now and hide."

But I settled down, took a deep breath and greeted the pack as they came across the finish line. They were upset and angry. I apologized. I didn't make excuses. I accepted total responsibility.

At that point Steve Scott jumped in and said, "We are athletes; if we can't handle a little adversity on the road, we shouldn't be out there." All the other athletes had great respect for Steve, and his words immediately settled everyone down and saved the day for me.

From that day on Steve has been my hero and my friend.

Lynn Flanagan, co-race director of the Holiday Bowl Heart of San Diego 10K poses in front of her favorite tourist attraction: "the trolley."
Photos this page by Lois Schwartz

Then there was our memorable trip to Phoenix. The state of Arizona had recently held a Senior Olympics, which was a huge event. The governor was interested in talking to us about doing a similar event in Southern California. He invited Ellen and I to come to the Governor's Luncheon, where he would honor all the people who had worked on his Olympic event. He wanted us to meet a lot of people and go to see the Suns basketball game. He paid for our plane tickets and our hotel room at the Ritz Carlton. This was during the time when we had no money. But we thought since they were paying for everything, we should go, so we did.

Someone from the governor's staff met us at the airport. As he dropped us off, he told us that we were invited to the Suns game that night, but all their staff would be busy and couldn't pick us up. No problem. "You should take a cab and put it on your hotel bill. You'll just need to show them your credit card." Oh, no—we didn't have a credit card.

Getting to the luncheon was no problem because it was held in our hotel. But all afternoon we fretted about how we were going to travel the distance from our hotel to the basketball game, out of range of the free hotel shuttle. We couldn't take a cab because we didn't have any money so we checked on the bus line and found we had enough change to take a bus.

As we walked by the doorman he offered to call us a cab. Our response was, "No. We're just going for a walk." And when we were out of his line of vision, we hopped on the next bus headed our way.

The next day we had a wait until our flight home. Ellen and I went for a long walk. She had forgotten running shoes, and after an hour of walking in sandals, she was a mess. Far from our hotel and with major blisters, no Band-Aids and again no money, we were in a bind. We finally walked into a different hotel, acted as though we were staying there, and asked for Band-Aids. A kind desk clerk bandaged her up, and we hobbled back the distance to our hotel where we waited for the governor's office to pick us up and take us to the airport.

One night I got a call from my staff. They had gone to our storage unit in Solana Beach late one night to load up for an event the next morning. The truck was loaded, but in the time it took them to load it, the business had closed for the night locking inside my staff and the truck with all the supplies until the next morning when the facility reopened. They were panicked! So I had to get out of bed, go to the storage unit where I met the fire department to verify that our team was legitimate and were not breaking in. Tragedy averted!

The Buick 10K was a classy event. Our client wanted their cars everywhere. They had a big sales event built around the race that proved to be quite effective. I got to drive a beautiful new Buick for six months, and then they decided to get at least one hundred new Buicks driven just for the race and then sold as a used car. All of my family, all of my friends, and all of the invited athletes drove these cars for a week or two. Then they were returned and sold as the official cars of the Buick 10K. Everyone loved it, and there were no problems until they all had to be returned. After some frantic phone calls, only one car was missing. We couldn't find it anywhere. We knew who had been assigned that car but couldn't find him anywhere.

After an exhaustive search, someone in our office decided to search the airport, and there it was, just sitting there. The runner who had been assigned that car had driven it to the airport and got on the plane to go back to his home state or country and didn't bother to tell anyone.

Fifteen

LETTING GO

As we entered the twenty-first century, we celebrated our twentieth year in business. We were solid. We were a company based on integrity, personal as well as corporate. We maintained the highest standards and insisted that our staff members do the same. Our calendar was full of quality events, and there were many more that we had to turn down because we were just too busy.

Our lease was up on the office we had rented for a number of years, and we decided maybe it was time to consider buying an office. We looked at lots of possibilities and then Travis found us the perfect spot in Bressi Ranch in Carlsbad. Christine redesigned the entire interior. It's beautiful. We have our own gym, a complete kitchen, a large conference room and a huge warehouse. I had a beautiful office upstairs with a couch and a TV and even a bit of ocean view. But I found I wasn't spending quite as much time in my office as I had in the past.

I was getting older and I occasionally thought about retiring, but I was quite certain I would never want to do that. What would I do all day? I was so used to being in the office by 7:00 a.m., usually before anyone else, and was the last to leave at the end of the day. I was on the phone or in meetings all day.

A Life in Motion

How was I going to fill up all that time up? I thought about art. I had always loved art and had taken a couple of classes many, many years ago when I was in high school and found I had some talent. When Katie and Pat were babies, I signed up for a life drawing class at Mission Bay High School. I was excited about doing this. Most of the people in the class were real artists with quite a bit of experience. The instructor was also very experienced. I thought this would be perfect for me until the end of the first evening, when the instructor informed us that each of us would be required to serve as a model for the other students to paint. There would be no exceptions and each one of us had to do this at least once and in the nude. I was horrified. I gathered up my equipment, ran out the door, and I never came back.

In more recent years my interest in painting was reignited. I found other art classes, those where you could keep your clothes on. I took many classes, covered our walls with my paintings, even had a few art shows where my paintings were sold. Travis was very interested in my painting and was quick to critique everything I did. One day I got a little annoyed, so I handed him a brush and an empty canvas and said "Do it your way." He struggled for a couple weeks, but soon got better and better and today is a very talented artist.

Around this time in life, he and I had started to do more traveling - Alaska at first, and then on to places like Budapest, Cairo, Jerusalem, Berlin, and Amsterdam. We had moved into a new home in La Costa so I had plenty to do and I was getting close to Social Security time, but I still couldn't imagine myself retiring. I would try to imagine what a day without working would be like. I would try to plan a whole day but could never get beyond 10:00 a.m. "Retirement" was a bad word for me. I had always been an avid reader and thought some day when I had more time I might join a book club. So I did and liked it well enough that I helped to start a book club in my neighborhood.

Lynn and Travis

Eleven years later, this club is alive and well. There is very little gossip, just lively discussion and of course good food and wine.

During the time I was considering whether to retire I had lunch with Barbie, a member of my original book club. She and I had become good friends and really had a lot in common. We talked about a book I had just read, about what to do with yourself after retiring. We ended up putting together a group of bright, well-educated women who were also considering retirement. They included three teachers, school principal, judge, and three business owners. We bonded immediately, and our regular gatherings were always stimulating and helpful. It turned out that we were all very liberal—very left-wing. We could spend hours trying to figure out how to save the world. We call ourselves No Red Hats. We do not want to be confused with the women's groups who go to lunch together in big red hats and bright purple dresses.

We have all retired now but are still at it—still trying to save the world.

While this was going on, my two daughters, Christine and Ellen, were starting to push a little bit for me to retire. To satisfy them, I agreed to put together a list of all the tasks I would still be responsible for.

I tried, but the list was huge and included things like all the sales, marketing, public relations, finances, elite athletes, charities. and the like. So they sent me back to try again. It took me several years to get a list that worked for the three of us.

On May 15, 2009, I formally stepped down turned over the reigns to Christine and Ellen. My new title became past President, Founder.

For the first few months I came to staff meetings, went to some client meetings and read reports regularly. For a while I played an advisory role in business development, budgeting and marketing. I was a regular in the office, but soon began to spend more time running or walking or having lunch with friends. I even served as a volunteer patient advocate at Tri-City Medical Center in Oceanside, twice a week.

It got to the point when the only time I was in the office was when I was working out with John, our personal trainer, twice a week or when there was a dinner meeting for the Tri-City Medical Center Carlsbad Marathon Race Committee.

"It runs in the family"
Pictured from left to right, Katie, Christine, Lynn and Ellen

That's when I had to admit it, I was retired! It's been nine years now since Christine and Ellen took over, and they continue to do a wonderful job. Katie continues to oversee all our In Motion Fit training programs and is still recognized as one of the best running coaches in Southern California. We can always count on Pat to help out at all our events. And when he has an event at his own Butterfly Farm, we help him.

Sixteen

ROADBLOCKS WON'T STOP ME

I have always been very healthy. Never any serious illnesses, not even the flu when everyone else got it. I was never overweight and I was still running in my mid-seventies. Those questionnaires you can take online indicated that I would probably live to be 106 years old.

At first I thought that was great, but then I wondered, who will I hang out with at 106 years old?

Then one day, I was finishing a very nice, relaxed five-mile run when I found myself flat on my face on the sidewalk. Wow! How did that happen?

I raised my head to see what had stopped me and all I saw was a flat sidewalk and lots of blood. "This is embarrassing, I have to get up and get home before anyone sees me." Several cars passed me without even noticing the woman lying on the sidewalk, but after about ten minutes, a very nice woman stopped and insisted on driving me home, even though I was bleeding all over her car.

When Travis got home he insisted on taking me to the emergency room. Four hours later, after eight stitches on my forehead, a CT scan, X-rays of my neck and hand, came a stern admonition from the doctor: "Don't run anymore!"

I didn't run again for two weeks.

But once the stitches were out, the bruises had faded, and all the bandages were gone, I was back on the road. I love to run, and I thought I always would. A few stitches weren't going to stop me. Over the next two years, I got a little slower, but I still insisted on running at least five days a week. I have to admit I had a couple falls, one running on the deck of a river cruise sailing down the Rhine River.

Then came several falls in my own neighborhood, followed by trips to the emergency room, and a couple doctors who insisted on knowing why I was falling. I blamed it on my shoes or a crack in the sidewalk. One ER doctor insisted I see a neurologist at Scripps Green for a CT scan. The neurologist didn't find anything on the scan but as we were talking, she asked me how long I'd had the tremors. I looked down at my hands and said, "I've never noticed that."

"Come back in a year, and we will do a more thorough check. You may have Parkinson's." She didn't seem too concerned, and I wasn't either but as time passed, I became more aware of the tremors. When the year was up, I called Scripps for an appointment and was told that this doctor was working on a research project and was not seeing any patients at this time.

I shopped around, tried another doctor—nice but not very focused or knowledgeable. Then a new neurology center opened close to home. I did some research and learned the center had a young doctor with a specialty in Parkinson's.

After a thirty-minute session with this young Parkinson's specialist, it was confirmed that I had Parkinson's. I wasn't happy about it, but I knew there were lots of treatments for Parkinson's, and I wasn't going to let it change my life. The doctor started prescribing different medications every couple of weeks by phone.

Nothing helped. The tremors got worse. This went on for six months.

I was losing weight—sixteen pounds—and finally one morning I threw up at Peet's coffee shop. I called the doctor, and as usual she wasn't available. I didn't get to talk to her, so I told the receptionist, "Please give her a message. Tell her I will not take one more pill she prescribes."

The receptionist was horrified. "You can't do that! She will definitely call you tonight "

She didn't call that night. She didn't call the next night. She never called again, but she continued to send prescriptions into my pharmacy, and I continued to send them back.

Travis pushed me to see a neurologist at UCSD, a nationally renowned movement disorder specialist. Jack Case, a longtime friend of Travis's and mine, was recently diagnosed with MSA, a form of Parkinsonism, and was struggling with his symptoms. We had watched Jack go from a strong, healthy man, playing golf all over Scotland two years ago to being confined to a wheelchair and not being able to talk clearly a year later.

Dr. Litvan, Jack's doctor, is very popular, so it took me several months to get in to see her. I had a three-hour appointment with her and her team. There were seven or eight doctors and nurses in the room with us the entire time. I finally felt that someone not only understood what was going on with me, but also cared.

At the end of the session, she gave me a list of follow-ups and tests that needed to be done, and then she told Travis and I that she thought I had something other than regular Parkinson's, that I might have one of the rare Parkinsonisms, MSA. Over the next six weeks she arranged all the tests to confirm or hopefully to rule out MSA.

Lynn Flanagan

After six weeks of testing, Travis and I went back for my appointment with Dr. Litvan and her team. We were optimistic but a little nervous. She is a very warm, friendly person, and she entered the room with a smile. She greeted everyone, then she reached out to Travis and I and said, "I'm sorry I have to tell you this, but your tests confirm you have MSA."

We were in a state of shock. MSA is Multiple Systems Atrophy. It's a disease of the brain and the spinal cord. It's very rare, with about thirteen thousand sufferers in the United States. It's similar to Parkinson's in the early stages, but it's much more aggressive.

As soon as we got in the car, Travis called the kids and said, "We want you to come over for dinner tonight," and of course they did. We told them the news, we all cried and then we agreed that we are getting through this together and we were not giving up. We spent the rest of the evening as we always do—enjoying good food, good wine, laughing, and loving together.

Then it was a Saturday morning, January 2, 2016. We had just finished the holidays. My sister and Larry were staying with us for a few days, Travis was having coffee with his buddies in Del Mar, and I was out for a run through the neighborhood. I was just passing our friends Carol and Joe's house when I did one of my famous face plants. No idea how or why it happened, but there I was, flat on my face and a bloody mess. I got up, wiped the blood off, and realized this was my last run. I could not do this to my family anymore. It wasn't fair. They were spending too much time in the emergency room with me.

Hours later, on a gurney in the emergency room at UCSD, surrounded by my children and Travis, I told them, "I won't ever run again" and sadly, I have had to keep that promise.

Filling the void was a problem. I started walking and gradually increased my distance and increased my pace, but I still missed

92

that feeling of total exhaustion that I got from running. Then I stumbled on an article about a boxing class for people with Parkinson's, and it wasn't far from home.

Travis and I checked it out, met the coach, and signed me up. We met twice a week for ninety-minute sessions, and I loved it. The men outnumbered the women four-to-one but we held our own. We stretched, did squats and sit-ups and jumped rope, and then we boxed. We really boxed! I started saying jab-cross in my sleep. We all became great friends; we supported each other and understood when someone fell or was having a bad day and just couldn't keep up. We understood. And we all loved Coach John and his volunteer assistants.

I was sure I would box the rest of my life, but things happen. I ran into a good friend, Carlo Cecchetto, the CBS Channel 8 evening news anchor. He had heard about my Parkinson's and invited me to do an interview the following week. I was eager to do it! I wanted to remind women to never give up, to make sure they're getting the right diagnosis and seeing the right doctors.

The day before the interview was scheduled, I was driving home from boxing when I felt really weird. Not sure what it was, but when I got home and tried to explain the feeling to Travis I found I was having a very hard time talking. I thought it must be another symptom of MSA, but it seemed early for that. What do I do about the interview? I didn't want to give up the opportunity to talk about two issues that are so important to me.

I got through the interview the next day with the wonderful Jeff Zevely from Channel 8. I wasn't able to do much talking, but Travis, Christine, and Ellen were right there to fill in, and I was able to close with a stern reminder—"Don't give up"—and I finished with "Make sure you have the right doctor!"

Later that same afternoon, Channel 8 sent a camera crew to my boxing class so they could film me in action on the bag. I could fight, but I still couldn't talk.

A few days later I seemed to be coming out of it, but I went to UCSD for a CT scan just to make sure there was nothing else wrong. I've had enough CTs in my day to know that they are a quick—ten minutes, and you're out of there. This was different. After the scan, they kept me on the table for thirty minutes. I could see the two technicians talking together in their glassed-in office. Then they were talking to someone else on the phone, and finally one of the technicians came out of his office and asked me if my husband was with me. I knew right away something was wrong.

They brought Travis in and then the technicians and Travis rushed me to the emergency room, where I stayed for a short time. The next thing I knew I was in ICU, surrounded by doctors and nurses. I stayed there for three days. There were neuro checks every hour around the clock, CT scans every two hours, and even another MRI at 12:30 a.m. There was no rest.

The bottom line: I'd had a stroke and later had two more strokes over the next few weeks. The stroke team was amazing; I was never alone and one of my doctors was Dr. Huisa-Garate, a Vascular Neuologist. After more testing his diagnosis was Amyloid Angiopathy, which in English means very fragile vessels in my brain that can burst at any time. More importantly, what it really meant was I'd had two brain bleeds in different parts of my brain. I thought maybe something like superglue would take care of it, but no such luck. There is no cure and no treatment for this condition. The stroke team was adamant. No more boxing or anything strenuous.

There is no correlation between MSA and Amyloid Angiopathy; both have No Cure, No Treatment and No Medication that will help.

A Life in Motion

I'm not happy about having two rare fatal diseases that have no cure and no treatment, but I am not giving up. There are far worse things that can happen to people. I have a great family, a great husband, great friends, and I've had a wonderful life. I can still walk five or six miles a day, and I walk fast. But because I had a very serious fall four weeks ago the doctors have now insisted that I can no longer walk alone. While I can't box anymore, I sometimes volunteer at boxing. I help my friends get their gloves on, I stabilize their bag while they punch, and I encourage them to keep fighting.

I've lost much of the use of my right hand from my MSA, my writing hand, but my wonderful son-in-law, Chris Larson, has set me up with a new computer and Dragon, a dictation program. My left hand is now starting to cause problems.

My glaucoma, which I've had for over ten years, is now starting to cause problems. The doctor told me recently that if they can't control the pressure with more eye drops, I will have to have surgery on my eye.

My strokes have had some impact on my speech. I sometime have trouble finding a word especially when I'm tired, but don't we all?

Sometimes I think I'm falling apart. But so what? I talk and Dragon writes. Chris is only six minutes away, and when I have a computer problem (which I often do), he is here to fix it.

Because of Chris and Dragon, I can still write. And Travis is right there to remind me of all the things I want to tell you. While I may have slowed down, I am still In Motion.

Thanks for reading my book.

Lynn

Acknowledgments

There is no way I could have accomplished my little book without the assistance and patience of some very special people. I already mentioned my husband, Travis Burleson, and my son-in-law, Chris Larson, but I want to tell you a little more about the role they played in my book. Travis has been by my side every step of the way, reminding me of things that should be included and encouraging me to keep going. He's my number one fan and cried when he read the first draft.

Chris made it possible for me to be an author. My MSA has made it very difficult for me to type or write, so he took me to Best Buy to pick out the right computer and the software I needed, and then he taught me how to use it. He is always at my beck and call whenever I have a computer problem. And he is here within ten minutes.

My four children: Katie Johnson, Pat Flanagan, Ellen Larson, and Christine Adams. They walk with me, take me to doctors' appointments, stand by me in the emergency room, and visit me during an ICU stay. They laugh with me and even sometimes cry with me, but they are always there for me. Jenifer, my stepdaughter, has her own very serious health issues and yet she's always eager to help me.

My grandchildren never run out of hugs, and the older ones—Caleb, Hannah, Saralyn, Kadie, and Myles—are encouraging me every step of the way.

I have two friends who are real authors as well as real artists. They each have been so kind and patient in sharing a wealth of information with me - the one who knew practically nothing when I started this journey. John Burnett and Ron Newby have led me on the path to finish a book that has some value to readers.

Thanks to my wonderful book club. I love each one of you. I never get tired of hearing you ask, "When will we be able to read your book?"

And finally, thanks to all my friends and family who have not only encouraged me to write but also have stood by me as I fight my crazy diseases.

I love you.

Epilogue

It was September 2, 2017, when my little brother, Chris, just back from his summer home in Charlevoix, Michigan, called me and said, "Let's get together for breakfast tomorrow."

In spite of the difference in our ages (sixteen years), we have always been close. He has a beautiful home in Charlevoix, where he spends four or five months a year, and spends the rest of his time at his mansion in Heritage Estates near Rancho Bernardo.

Travis and I met with him at a favorite breakfast place in San Marcos. We hadn't seen each other for almost two months, so we had lots to talk about. I couldn't help but notice the tremor in his hands as we ate and talked. I didn't say anything until we had finished breakfast and started to leave the restaurant.

I hugged him and said, "Are you going to see a doctor about this?" His response was quick. "I already have. They think I have Parkinson's." My heart sank. How could this be? He was too young – only 60. He was too strong. Too healthy. He had everything!

"Can we talk?

"Yes," he said. "I want to talk to you about your doctor. I don't have much confidence in the doctors I have seen. Can I call you this afternoon?"

Since that day, we talk regularly, sometimes daily. So far none of the medications that several doctors have tried have worked for him. His tremors have gotten worse and he struggles to maintain balance. His symptoms are very similar to my early MSA, which scares both of us. He has very little patience and can't understand why doctors can't just fix his problem tomorrow.

Fortunately, he finally got an appointment with my doctor at UCSD, and it's coming up soon. In the meantime, we will continue our conversations, comparing tremors, difficulty sleeping, upset stomach, near falls, drooling. But we always have something to laugh about too. I think we both worry about each other. He told me recently that when he found out about my diagnosis, he cried. Then when he got his diagnosis, he cried again. So did I. I love my brother and I don't want him to have what I have. I can accept what has happened to me, but it's hard for me to accept it for him.

But whatever happens, we will deal with it. We are both strong and we can find joy every day. And of course, side by side, we will always find something to laugh about together.

Great news! Yesterday Chris finally met with Dr. Litvan, my doctor. After a three hour session with her and her associates she confirmed that he has Parkinson's but he does not have the MSA that I have. It was a tremendous relief for both of us.

Lynn's brother Chris (foreground) with daughter, Ellen

Lynn, Ellen and Christine in earlier years

Lynn at the 2018 Carlsbad Marathon Expo

Lynn and the 2018 Carlsbad Marathon pace car

Lynn-"another day at the office"

Lynn with a few of her granddogs, Duke and Love

Lynn and Travis reflecting on Lynn's brother Mark's life and passing

Chris and Lynn "We Did It!"